Frommer's®

MEMORABLE WALKS IN LONDON

3rd Edition

by Richard Jones

Victoria Mose

D1206367

MACMILLAN • USA

MACMILLAN TRAVEL
A Simon & Schuster Macmillan Company
1633 Broadway
New York, NY 10019

Find us online at **www.frommers.com.**

ISBN 0-02-862142-5
ISSN 1081-3365

Editor: Ron Boudreau
Production Editor: Lori Cates
Design by Amy Peppler Adams—designLab, Seattle
Digital Cartography by Roberta Stockwell and Ortelius Design

SPECIAL SALES
Bulk purchases (10+ copies) of Frommer's and selected Macmillan travel guides are available to corporations, organizations, mail-order catalogs, institutions, and charities at special discounts, and can be customized to suit individual needs. For more information write to Special Sales, Macmillan General Reference, 1633 Broadway, New York, NY 10019.

Manufactured in the United States of America.

Contents

LIST OF MAPS

• • • • • • •

About the Author

Richard Jones, who lives in the City, has been devising, researching, and conducting guided walking tours of London since 1982. Richard also lectures frequently on London's history to groups in the United States and Canada. He is a coauthor of *Frommer's Europe, Frommer's Europe from $50 a Day,* and *Frommer's Walking Tours: England's Favorite Cities.*

An Invitation to the Reader

In researching this book, we have come across many wonderful sights, pubs, and restaurants, the best of which we have included here. We are sure that many of you will also discover appealing places as you explore London. Please don't keep them to yourself. Share your experiences, especially if you want to bring to our attention information that has changed since this book was researched. You can address your letters to:

Frommer's Memorable Walks in London, 3rd Edition
Macmillan Travel
1633 Broadway
New York, NY 10019

An Additional Note

Please be advised that travel information is subject to change at any time. The authors, editors, and publisher cannot be held responsible for the experiences of readers while traveling. Your safety is important to us, however, so we encourage you to stay alert and be aware of your surroundings. Keep a close eye on cameras, purses, and wallets, all favorite targets of thieves and pickpockets.

Find Frommer's Online

Arthur Frommer's Outspoken Encyclopedia of Travel (www.frommers.com) offers more than 6,000 pages of up-to-the-minute travel information—including the latest bargains and candid, personal articles updated daily by Arthur Frommer himself. No other Web site offers such comprehensive and timely coverage of the world of travel.

Introducing the City by the Thames

Sprawling across 600-plus square miles, Greater London has been building, growing, and changing continuously for almost 2,000 years. The city's commercial core, the West End, is laid out with broad boulevards and huge palaces, reflecting the city's former status as the capital of a globe-spanning empire. When you leave the West End, however, you'll immediately note how diverse London has become for most of its 8 million residents. The centuries have shaped it into a complex amalgam of communities—a collection of towns, each with its own tradition and spirit.

The extreme mix of cultures—a relic of what was once known as the British Empire—gives London a certain depth of character that has long kept it at the forefront of the world's art, music, and fashion scenes. The ever-changing myriad of immigrant communities has constantly challenged and redefined London's character. Though less important than it once was, the British class system stubbornly endures. Royal London's pomp and pageantry may look increasingly like a tourist attraction, but daily ceremonies like the Changing of the Guard and the Ceremony of the Keys are striking reminders of an influential cultural heritage. Ironically, the scandal-ridden Royal Family appears to be symbolic of the nation's troubles.

Take advantage of London's terrific offerings and unique opportunities. Explore the narrow alleyways of the City, enjoy lunch at a local pub, attend a free concert at a church, and strike up a conversation with the locals. Though you may need to speak first, you'll generally find that Londoners are friendly and helpful. And they speak English. Sort of.

The 11 walking tours in this book are organized by either geographical area or topic. They'll take you off the main streets as much as possible—they'll lead you down unexpected passages and into secluded courtyards; introduce you to that most English of institutions, the pub; guide you through the streets of Dickens's London and show you the landmarks he might still recognize; and help you discover, all over the city, sites and corners you might not have found by yourself.

The approximate time each tour should take is specified. None of the walks is physically strenuous—each is designed to be accessible (and interesting) to all ages. Walk, look, listen, learn, and enjoy.

THE FOUNDING OF LONDON

Though scholars debate the origin of London's name, popular belief is that it comes from the Celtic *Llyn Din,* meaning "lakeside fortress."

When the Romans arrived in A.D. 43, they chose Londinium as the name for their settlement on the Thames. They built a bridge, and the town began to flourish around the north bank of the bridgehead. In the late 2nd century, the Romans erected a massive wall of Kentish ragstone around the city to protect it from attack by neighboring tribes, and you can still see remnants of it (see Walking Tour 1). Within a century, the population had increased to 15,000 and Londinium had become a bustling center of trade and industry. Roman Britain lasted until the late 3rd century, when Saxon invaders began to encroach on southern England. Meanwhile, Rome itself came under siege, and in A.D. 410 Londinium's Roman troops departed for home.

Over the next 400 years, various Germanic tribes, collectively called Anglo-Saxons, began to settle in England and by A.D. 871 were united under Alfred the Great, the first in the line of Saxon kings. He strengthened London's fortifications against the Vikings, whose raids were a constant threat. Edward the Confessor (1003–66), who was later to be canonized, transferred the court and the government from Winchester to Westminster. He rebuilt Westminster Abbey, and Harold II, the last of the Saxon rulers, was crowned there.

However, it was William the Conqueror who first understood the political importance of London and left an indelible mark on it. His 1066 coronation in Westminster Abbey established a precedent that has been followed ever since. He recognized London as the capital and allowed the City of London to continue electing its own leaders—a decision that was to have far-reaching consequences. English monarchs from that time on, eager for the support of the country's wealthiest people, strove to hold London as the key to controlling England. William also built the White Tower, which was later incorporated into the Tower of London.

By the 15th century, the banks of the Thames were lined with warehouses and great mansions built by the rising merchants. The population had grown to 30,000, and ecclesiastical establishments were flourishing (their names—Whitefriars, Blackfriars, Greyfriars—still remain part of London). The suburbs expanded beyond the City's walls and many new ones were created; however, since there was no central planning, the roads developed haphazardly, creating the confusing street pattern that still exists today.

THE ADVENT OF MODERN LONDON

Modern London began with the Tudors. Henry VIII built St. James's Palace and enclosed what is now Hyde Park and Green Park for his private grounds. His Reformation and the dissolution of the monasteries led to the destruction of many medieval ecclesiastical buildings. The church's wealth was confiscated and redistributed to a new aristocracy that supported the monarch; among those who were executed for refusing to acknowledge Henry's supremacy as head of the church was the internationally prominent man of letters Sir Thomas More, author of *Utopia*.

The ascension of Elizabeth I ushered in an era of peace and prosperity. Elizabethan England was a period of unparalleled creativity. Poetry, theater, and spectacle flourished. Open-air playhouses, including Shakespeare's Globe Theatre, were built in the borough of Southwark (the city fathers had puritanically banned theaters in the belief that they attracted the wrong element).

The Tours at a Glance

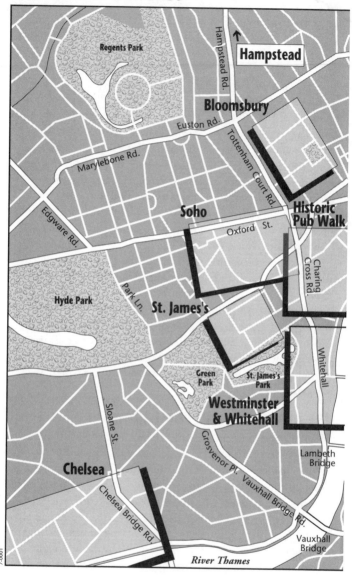

Plays by Shakespeare, Ben Jonson, and Christopher Marlowe were performed there. Along with the flowering of the arts, England had entered a period of colonial and mercantile expansion in rivalry with Spain, and London was a prime beneficiary.

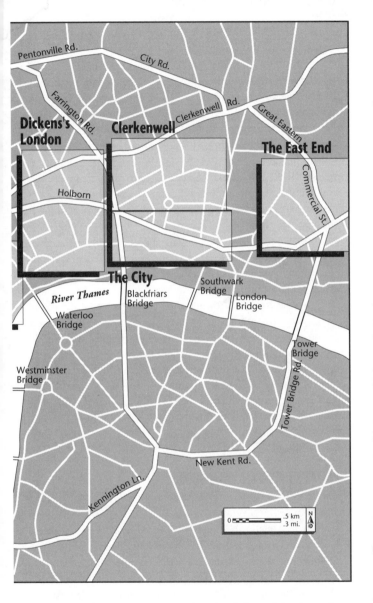

All these trends continued after the defeat of the Spanish Armada and into the Jacobean period. John Donne's poetry and John Webster's tragic dramas built upon literary and dramatic traditions. Inigo Jones (1573–1652), generally viewed as the first modern British architect, introduced Palladian style into

London and built the Queen's House at Greenwich and the Banqueting House at Whitehall.

During this time the conflict between the Stuart kings and the Puritans steadily intensified, but religion was not the only issue. The king claimed the privileges of a divine-right monarch against a parliament that advocated constitutional monarchy. After the Puritan victory in 1649, Charles I stepped through the window of the Banqueting Hall and onto the scaffold where he lost his head.

In the years that followed, the arts were rigorously suppressed and many of the important Gothic cathedrals damaged—stained glass was smashed and religious artifacts were destroyed. Though the great poet John Milton supported the Puritans, he published his most noted works, *Paradise Lost* and *Samson Agonistes,* after the restoration of Charles II in 1660.

Although plague had long been endemic in London, it didn't attain epidemic proportions until 1665, when tens of thousands died in what became known as the "Great Plague." In the next year, medieval London was destroyed by the Great Fire. Fanned by strong easterly winds, it burned more than 10,000 buildings, taking with it the crowded and unsanitary half-timbered buildings that had helped to spread the plague. After the fire, houses were rebuilt of stone and brick. Christopher Wren, who was commissioned to redesign the city, then built his masterpieces: St. Paul's Cathedral and St. Mary-le-Bow, Chelsea Royal Hospital, Kensington Palace, and dozens of other London buildings.

18TH-CENTURY LONDON

In the 18th century, England was transformed into a world-class financial and military power, and London again became the primary beneficiary of the new prosperity. This was the great era of Georgian architecture, which you can still see in Grosvenor, Bedford, and Hanover squares, as well as in other London squares and streets. The Georgian style spilled over into the applied arts, including furniture, silver, and glass. The great porcelain works and potteries of Wedgwood, Spode, and Staffordshire were established at this time. Two new bridges—Blackfriars and Westminster—were built, streets upgraded, and hospitals improved. A number of painters gained prominence, including Joshua Reynolds, Thomas Gainsborough, and William Hogarth; and several noteworthy sculptors, like Grinling Gibbons, emerged. Samuel Johnson compiled his famous dictionary, James Boswell wrote his great biography of the lexicographer/critic, and David Garrick performed his memorable Shakespearean roles at his playhouse in Drury Lane (often changing Shakespeare's tragic endings to happy ones to suit the temper of the times). The new wealth produced by the Industrial Revolution led to the emergence of a middle class that soon partly merged with and bolstered the older land-owning aristocracy.

VICTORIAN LONDON

Queen Victoria ascended the throne in 1837 and reigned for 64 years—the longest tenure in English history. Since the new middle class believed that education was essential to prosperity, the University of London and free municipal public libraries were established. The National Gallery at Trafalgar Square was completed in 1838, and the British Museum's new building in Bloomsbury was finished in 1857. At this time, progress changed the face of London, transforming it into a modern metropolis as rail lines and steam engines, underground trains, sewage systems, and new building techniques greatly expanded its borders. Buckingham Palace was enlarged and sheathed in honey-colored stone, and the Gothic extravagance of the Albert Memorial defined an architectural style that only recently has begun to be appreciated.

Victorian London was the center of the largest empire the world had ever seen. Londoners traveled all over the globe to fill military and administrative posts. This period is the one that still influences our present-day view of London and of the English: It was shaped by the growing power of the bourgeoisie, the queen's moral stance, and the perceived responsibilities of managing an empire. The racy London of the preceding three centuries moved underground. Meanwhile, in the poorer neighborhoods the dialects and attitudes (later referred to as "cockney") were developing. The cockney humor of London's vaudeville and music halls influenced the entertainment industry from Sydney to San Francisco.

The outbreak of World War I marked the end of an era: Until then it had been widely assumed that peace, progress, prosperity, empire, and, incidentally, social improvement would continue indefinitely. Following World War I came 2 decades of social unrest and political uncertainty, both at home and throughout the empire.

WORLD WAR II & POSTWAR LONDON

During World War II, London suffered repeated bombings, and almost every notable building was seriously damaged. Trenches were dug in public parks, and the Underground stations doubled as bomb shelters. The heroism and stoicism with which this ordeal was endured is still a nostalgic memory to Londoners as well as a source of local pride.

Since the 12th century, the City of London has been governed by an independent corporation headed by the Lord Mayor. In 1986, authority was replaced by a division of governing responsibility between the central government and the boroughs. Modern office structures, centrally heated apartment buildings, and successive waves of immigrants have literally and figuratively changed the face of contemporary London. Many tourists are disappointed when they first arrive because the past isn't immediately or easily visible, but if they scratch the surface they'll find a complex city that's an amalgam of all the preceding eras. One of London's most colorful pageants—the Lord Mayor's Procession and Show—derives from the ancient right of the City of London corporation to require the monarch to ask the Lord Mayor's permission to enter the City's original square mile.

The City's tangle of streets originated as paths during the Middle Ages. Several buildings from the 15th century still stand, including Guildhall (see Walking Tour 1) and Southwark Cathedral. Throughout London you'll find examples of Tudor and Stuart architecture, designed in the English Renaissance style, with Italian and French models (themselves inspired by the architecture of classical Greece and Rome). Banqueting House (see Walking Tour 4), St. Paul's Cathedral (see Walking Tour 1), and the Chelsea Royal Hospital (see Walking Tour 10) are three distinctive examples. Though most of the structures from London's past are long gone, those eras are recalled in street names. Bucklesbury and Lothbury refer to the *buhrs* (stone mansions) of Norman barons. Ludgate, Aldgate, and Cripplegate refer to ancient gates of the City wall. The word *Barbican* derives from the watch tower that once stood in its place. In the Middle Ages "cheaps" were markets—hence, the origin of names like Eastcheap and Cheapside. Some streets bear the names of products formerly sold there—look for Milk Street, Bread Street, and Friday Street (where fish was sold).

The City

Start: Bank Underground Station.

Finish: St. Paul's Underground Station.

Time: 2½ to 3 hours.

Best Time: Weekdays from 10am to 4pm.

Worst Time: Nights and weekends, when many buildings are closed.

T he City of London, occupying approximately 1 square mile, was established by the Romans, who erected a protective wall around it in the 2nd century A.D. During the Middle Ages a series of gates was built to facilitate entry into the City; these are now commemorated in street names like New Gate and Alders (older) Gate. Other street names in the City derive from the goods and services that were traded there, like Bread Street, Wood Street, and even Love Lane.

In the early Middle Ages, the City asserted its independence from royal jurisdiction; it established an autonomous government with a Lord Mayor and a court of aldermen (elders). Today, the City remains both England's financial center and an autonomous precinct. On certain local matters it creates and enforces its own laws. Many of the winding, narrow streets have changed little over the centuries, making this part of London one of the most interesting for strolling.

• • • • • • • • • • • • • • • •

Leave Bank Underground Station via the Royal Exchange exit. At this intersection in the City you'll be able to see several of Britain's most important financial institutions. Directly outside the exit is the:

1. **Royal Exchange,** founded by Sir Thomas Gresham in the mid-16th century for the purpose of trading wholesale and retail goods. The present building, designed by Sir William Tite, dates from 1844. Since 1972, when world currencies were floated, this building has been the head-quarters for the London International Financial Futures Exchange (LIFFE).

   The large neoclassical building across Threadneedle Street is the:

2. **Bank of England,** designed by Sir John Soane and built between 1788 and 1833. A new complex was added by Sir Herbert Baker between the two World Wars. Known as the "Old Lady of Threadneedle Street," this is a central bank—managing the public debt and serving as a depository for government funds—as well as the institution that issues bank notes for general circulation.

   The bank was established "for the Publick Good and Benefit of Our People" in 1694, when a Royal Charter was granted by William III and Mary II. Though it carried out government functions, the bank remained privately owned until 1946.

   If you'd like to visit the **Bank of England Museum** (☎ 0171/601-4878), cross Threadneedle Street and turn right. Take the first left into Bartholomew Lane, where you'll find the museum entrance on the left.

   Retrace your steps to the front of the Royal Exchange. Cross over Cornhill, where, in the middle of the street, you'll see a **statue commemorating J. H. Greathead.** He invented the traveling shield, which made it possible to cut the tunnels of London's Underground system.

   On the opposite side of Cornhill, proceed into Popes Head Alley, at the end of which turn right into Lombard Street. Cross the road, continue right toward the traffic lights, and then follow the sidewalk left. Take the first left turn into Mansion House Place. On the right is:

3. **Mansion House,** the official residence of the Lord Mayor, built by George Dance the Elder between 1739 and 1753. The Corinthian columns form an impressive backdrop for the Lord Mayor's appearance at ceremonial functions. The main reception room, Egyptian Hall, is the setting for official banquets. Alas, Mansion House is closed to the public.

   Continue along the right side of Mansion House Place and enter the little passage called St. Stephen's Row. At its end, turn left into **Walbrook.** This street is named for the brook around which the Romans built their original London settlement. By the 14th century, the brook had become polluted and work was begun to cover it over. By the 16th century, no further trace of it remained. Immediately on your left is the entrance to the:

4. **Church of St. Stephen Walbrook.** This may be not only the finest church designed by Wren but also London's most beautiful church. *The Critical Review of Publick Buildings in London* (1734) observed that it was "famous all over Europe and justly reputed the masterpiece of the celebrated Sir Christopher Wren. Perhaps Italy itself can produce no modern buildings that can vie with this in taste or proportion."

   The **altar,** at the church's center, was carved by Henry Moore. When the rector, Chad Varah (who founded the Samaritans in the 1950s), asked the sculptor to create an altar, Moore claimed that he was an agnostic. Chad replied, "Henry, I'm not asking you to take the service. I understand that you're a bit of a chiseler; just do your job."

   Exit the church, cross Walbrook, and proceed into Bucklesbury. Walk straight ahead and turn left into Queen Victoria Street. One block farther, turn left and go up the steps outside the main entrance of Temple Court. Turn left and stop by the railings to look at the:

5. **Temple of Mithras,** Queen Victoria Street. Mithraism, an ancient Persian cult that was introduced to London by Roman soldiers, became widely accepted during the 2nd century. The temple was built in the 3rd century, when the religion was at the height of its popularity. Probably it was destroyed in the 4th century, when the Roman Empire under Constantine accepted Christianity (many pagan temples were torn down at that time). The temple's former entrance

The City

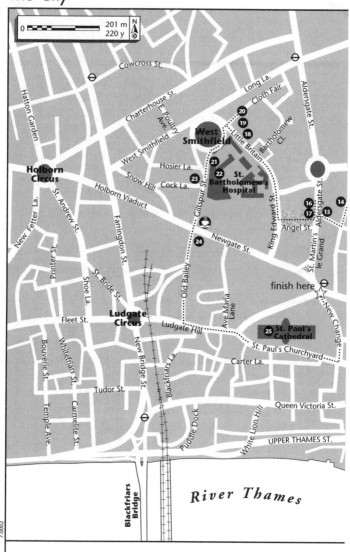

1. Royal Exchange
2. Bank of England
3. Mansion House
4. Church of St. Stephen Walbrook
5. Temple of Mithras
6. Ye Olde Watling
7. St. Mary-le-Bow Church
8. Cheapside
9. Wood Street
10. Guildhall
11. Bust of William Shakespeare
12. St. Olave's Silver Street
13. Site of the Christopher Mountjoy House
14. Roman Fort

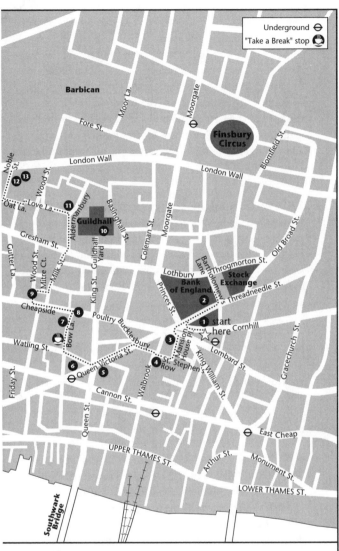

- **15** Museum of London
- **16** St. Botolph's Church
- **17** Postman's Park
- **18** Gatehouse of
  St. Bartholomew the Great
- **19** Church of
  St. Bartholomew the Great
- **20** Cloth Fair
- **21** Henry VIII Gateway
- **22** Church of
  St. Bartholomew
  the Less
- **23** Fat Boy
- **24** Old Bailey Courthouse
- **25** St. Paul's Cathedral

is to your right at the end of the central nave (lined with columns dividing it into aisles). The temple was discovered in 1954 when developers were excavating a new building site. Sculptures and other objects from the temple are now on display at the Museum of London.

Return to the top of the steps outside Temple Court. To the left you'll have a great view of St. Paul's Cathedral. To its left is a red telephone box. Cross Queen Victoria Street and make your way to the telephone box on Watling Street. Proceed along Watling for half a block; on your left you'll come to:

6. Ye Olde Watling, 29 Watling St. (☎ **0171/248-6252**). Built in 1668 by Sir Christopher Wren, this atmospheric old pub was constructed with wood taken from dismantled sailing ships. The pub served as Wren's office during the construction of nearby St. Paul's Cathedral. Good lunches are available here, as well as Bass, IPA, Best Bitter, and other beers. You can stop for a break here or wait for the next stop.

Cross Watling Street onto **Bow Lane,** a charming little pedestrian thoroughfare that evokes the medieval period. Before the 16th century, this lane was called Cordwainers Street, named for the shoemakers and leather workers who lived and traded here, but then it was renamed for the nearby church.

A few steps down Bow Lane, turn left into covered Groveland Court to find:

Take a Break **Williamson's Tavern** (☎ **0171/248-6280**). In the 17th century, this was the official residence of the Lord Mayor of the City of London. The wrought-iron gates in front were presented to the Lord Mayor by William III (1650–1702) and Mary II (1662–94). Inside, you'll see a fireplace constructed of ancient Roman tiles that were discovered on this site when the pub was erected. The tavern is famous with locals for its terrific steak sandwiches.

Retrace your footsteps to Bow Lane and turn left. After another half a block, turn left into Bow Churchyard. Turn right, into the main churchyard, and then right again through the gates to descend into the crypt of:

7. **St. Mary-le-Bow Church.** In the crypt you can see the remains of previous churches that formerly existed on this site, as well as the arches (or bows) for which Bow Lane was named.

   Exit the crypt and turn right into Bow Churchyard. On your right is the church entrance. Traditionally, an authentic cockney was defined as someone born within hearing range of the Bow bells. The first mention of this church traces back to 1091, when it was recorded that the roof blew off in a storm—the beginning of what seemed to be a string of bad luck. In 1196, William Fitz Osbert was smoked out of the church's tower after murdering one of the Archbishop of Canterbury's guards. In 1271, the tower fell, killing 20 people. In 1284, a local goldsmith was murdered in this church. In 1331, the collapse of a balcony on which Queen Phillipa (wife of Edward III) was standing injured her and several of her attendants. Finally, the church was burned in the Great Fire of 1666. Rebuilt by Wren, the present building was modeled after Rome's Church of the Basilica of Maxentius. The 217-foot steeple is widely considered Wren's finest. Inside, look at the arches flanking the nave, each surmounted by a stone relief of the World War II allied heads of state, including Winston Churchill, Charles de Gaulle, and Franklin D. Roosevelt.

   Exit the church and look at the **statue of Capt. John Smith,** a parishioner of St. Mary-le-Bow and one of the first colonists to settle Jamestown, Virginia. Smith may have been responsible for the early survival of the first permanent English settlement in North America because of his adaptability to the new environment and his leadership. In his written accounts, he described the beauty and natural resources of the New World.

   Turn left into the street in front of the church:

8. **Cheapside,** formerly one of London's busiest commercial streets. From the 13th to the 17th century this thoroughfare was a bustling marketplace for jewelry, shoes, bread, meat, spices, wine, and all kinds of trinkets and supplies. Its name derives from the Anglo-Saxon word *ceap* (or *chepe*), meaning "to barter." This is the origin of the modern word *cheap,* and *shopping* evolved from the word *cheping*.

Cheapside's timber-framed shops were destroyed by the Great Fire, after which the street was widened and lined with loftier buildings. The expansion of London in the late 18th and 19th centuries gave rise to a rival area—Oxford Street, which is now one of the city's most important shopping streets.

Cautiously cross Cheapside and continue to the left. One block ahead, turn right into:

9. **Wood Street,** London's former timber-selling center. Look up at the large **plane tree** on your left at the corner of Cheapside. This tree was immortalized by the Romantic poet William Wordsworth in "The Reverie of Poor Susan":

> *At the corner of Wood Street*
> *when daylight appears*
> *Hangs a thrush that sings loud,*
> *It has sung for three years.*
> *Poor Susan has passed by the*
> *spot, and has heard*
> *In the silence of morning,*
> *the song of the bird.*

Take the first right turn into Milk Street and follow it around to the left. Proceed ahead and turn right into Gresham Street. Cross the street and make your way to the Church of St. Lawrence Jewry. Turn left by the church and proceed into the courtyard of:

10. **Guildhall** (☎ 0171/606-3030), the City of London's City Hall and the seat of the Lord Mayor and the Court of Aldermen since the 12th century. The present building was completed in 1439 but was severely damaged in the Great Fire and again by German bombers in December 1940.

Inside the hall, look back at the entrance door. On the right side is **Gog** and on the left **Magog.** According to legend, these two ferocious-looking giants represent warriors in the conflict between the ancient inhabitants of Britain and Trojan invaders. The outcome of their conflict was the establishment of New Troy, reputedly on the site of present-day London. With your back to the giants, look left to the **statue of Winston Churchill,** unveiled on June 21, 1955.

At the far end of the hall, beside the doorway on the left,

is a board listing some of the trials that have taken place here. Included is the name of **Dr. Roderigo Lopez,** a Portuguese Jew who served as physician to Elizabeth I. He was accused of (and later executed for) trying to poison the queen. As one of the most despised citizens of his day, Lopez may have been the model for Shylock in Shakespeare's *Merchant of Venice.*

Exit Guildhall and turn right (just before the church); pass under the offices and turn right onto Aldermanbury. Two doors along on your right is the entrance to the **Guildhall Library.** Open Monday to Saturday from 9:30am to 5pm, it contains excellent source material on British (especially London) history. This is also the entrance to the **Clock Museum,** which displays exhibits on the history of clock making.

Continue along Aldermanbury and cross over at Love Lane, to the garden where you can see a:

11. **Bust of William Shakespeare,** commemorating John Heminge and Henry Condell—fellow actors and personal friends of Shakespeare who lived for many years in this parish. They collected all Shakespeare's known works and arranged for the publication of the first folio of his plays in 1623. As inscribed on the monument: "They thus merited the gratitude of mankind." Behind the bust are the remains of the **Church of St. Mary Aldermanbury,** which was dismantled in the 1960s and reassembled at Westminster College in Fulton, Missouri, as a memorial to Winston Churchill.

    Continue along **Love Lane,** once a notorious red-light district named for the services sold there. Cross Wood Street and proceed into the covered passageway called St. Alban's Court. Turn right into Oat Lane and, a block later, right into Noble Street. At the end of the block is a small garden, with the remains of:

12. **St. Olave Silver Street.** Go up the steps and follow the pathway. Pause at the top of the next set of steps and look to your right. Though the land here is empty, it may be one of London's most interesting literary sites, for it is the:

13. **Site of the Christopher Mountjoy House.** A Frenchman, Mountjoy made wigs and fashionable headdresses.

He lived at the corner of the former Silver and Monkwell streets with his wife, his daughter, an apprentice named Stephen Bellott, and a lodger named William Shakespeare. The parents wanted their daughter to marry the apprentice, and Mme Mountjoy persuaded Shakespeare to act as matchmaker. He was successful and the marriage took place at the Church of St. Olave Silver Street on November 19, 1604. Mme Mountjoy died a few years later, and a dispute arose between Stephen Bellott and his father-in-law. In 1612, Bellott brought suit against Mountjoy in the Court of Requests in an attempt to recover £60. One of the witnesses summoned to give evidence was Shakespeare. From his evidence and the testimony of other witnesses who referred to him, we've been able to learn something of Shakespeare's personal life in London. He lived with the Mountjoys for 6 years before the wedding and probably for several more afterward. While living here, Shakespeare wrote perhaps 10 plays.

Retrace your footsteps to Noble Street. Cross over to the building marked **1 London Wall** to look at some of the remains of the city wall. The wall is of Roman origin up to a height of about 8 feet; the remainder was added during the medieval period.

Facing the wall, walk left along Noble Street; at the end of the railings, look down at the remains of the:

14. **Roman Fort,** one of London's oldest structures. Built around A.D. 120, the fort originally covered 12 acres and accommodated the guards of the Roman Governor of Britain. At least 1,000 men were housed in the barracks. These remaining walls were part of the curved southwest corner watch tower.

Continue to the end of Noble Street and turn right into Gresham Street. One block later, turn right and continue to the pedestrian crossing; cross Aldersgate Street. To the right is the:

15. **Museum of London** (☎ 0171/600-3699), which houses artifacts excavated along much of this walk, elucidating much of London's past. It's open Tuesday to Saturday from 10am to 5:50pm and Sunday from noon to 5:50pm. There's an admission charge.

Here on Aldersgate Street, you're at:

16. **St. Botolph's Church,** one of three City churches dedicated to the patron saint of travelers. Each St. Botolph church is near the former site of a City gate—in this case, Aldersgate. If the church is open, you can explore its interesting interior, complete with a splendid barrel-vaulted roof and a sword rest for the Lord Mayor's sword of state.

    Walk through the gate to the left of the church to enter:

17. **Postman's Park,** named for its proximity to the General Post Office. Walk straight ahead to the small monument with the red terra-cotta roof. This is a national memorial commemorating acts of heroism by ordinary men and women. Dedicated in 1910, the monument is covered with epitaphs to unsung heroes such as John Cranmer, age 23, who "drowned off Ostend whilst saving the life of a stranger and a foreigner."

    Continue straight through the park and exit via the gate opposite the one you entered. Turn right onto Little Britain, cross at the pedestrian crossing, and continue right for 3 blocks to the:

18. **Gatehouse of St. Bartholomew the Great,** at Smithfield Square. Take a step back to admire this stunning old church entrance. Above the gate is one of the earliest surviving timber-frame house fronts in London. It was built by William Scudamore in 1595 and restored in 1916 after damage from a zeppelin bomb. Parts of the stone gate date from 1240, but most of the stonework was installed during a restoration in 1932.

    Walk through the gatehouse and straight into the:

19. **Church of St. Bartholomew the Great,** London's oldest parish church, part of an Augustinian priory founded in 1123 by a monk named Rahere. The church was spared from the Great Fire as well as World War II bombing. Just inside the door, on your right, are the church's 15th-century cloisters.

    Continue along the right aisle of the church and pause by the second radiator on your right. Look up at the **monument to Edward Cooke,** a philosopher and Doctor of Physick who died in 1652. The marble from which the statue is made condenses water from the air in wet weather—thus, it "weeps." (The inscription asks you to watch for this.)

Go to the central aisle and face the main altar. To the left is the **tomb of Rahere.** Rahere had been a courtier at the court of Henry I, but when the heir to the throne drowned at sea, Rahere became a monk. Later, on a pilgrimage to Rome, he came down with malaria. He vowed that if God cured him, he'd return to London and build a church. Following his cure, he was on his way home when he had a dream in which St. Bartholomew told him to go to "the smoothfield without the city gates and build there a church, hospital, and monastery."

With your back to the main altar, look up to your left at the lovely oriel window, called the **Prior Bolton's Window.** As prior from 1506 to 1532, Bolton had his quarters behind this window, which he had constructed so that he could watch the monks at their service. Beneath the central pane is his rebus—a pictorial representation of his name—dating from a time when most people could neither read nor write. This one depicts a crossbow bolt piercing a wine barrel (or tun), meaning "Bolt tun."

Cross to the far aisle and turn left. Pause by the second window on the right. To the left of two enormous jugs is the **monument to John and Margaret Whiting,** a couple who died within a year of each other. The inscription ends with these lines:

Shee first deceased, hee for a little Tryd
To live without her, Liked it not and dyd.

In 1539, Henry VIII confiscated all this church's property, which was then used for stables, a private home, and a printing office where Benjamin Franklin worked in 1725.

Exit the church from the same door you entered; go up the churchyard steps and exit via the gate in the far right corner. The street ahead is:

20. **Cloth Fair,** site of the Bartholomew Fair, a sort of medieval street carnival held annually from 1123 to 1855. The gabled houses opposite date from 1604 and are thus among the few examples of buildings that predate the Great Fire.

Immediately after these buildings, turn right into Cloth Court and look up at the wall on the left. Here you'll see the **Sailors Home Coming Window.** To the right of this is a blue plaque commemorating the fact that Sir John Betjeman (1906–84), the Poet Laureate, lived here.

Continue along Cloth Fair and turn left into West Smithfield. To your right is **Smithfield Market** (see Stop 4 in Walking Tour 7).

As you continue along West Smithfield, notice how the wall on your left is somewhat pockmarked. This damage was caused in 1916 by shrapnel when a zeppelin dropped a bomb on the square. Farther along on the left is the:

21. **Henry VIII Gateway,** built free of charge in 1702 by the stonemasons who constructed St. Paul's Cathedral. Above it is the only statue to Henry VIII in London, commemorating the fact that, following his dissolution of the monasteries, he gave the hospital to the city of London.

Go through the gateway a little distance; on the left you'll come to the entrance to the:

22. **Church of St. Bartholomew the Less.** The hospital became its own parish in 1546, when Henry VIII gave the hospital to the city of London. This is the only hospital parish church in existence. Note the two 15th-century arches that survive under the Tower. Go up the steps to your left; just in front of the wooden screen, pull back the green carpet to see the 14th-century **Markeby Brass,** a memorial to William and Alice Markeby. This is one of the few accessible remaining brasses in a London church. When you leave, be sure to replace the carpet over the brass.

Exit the church and retrace your footsteps to the main gate. Turn left into Giltspur Street. One block farther on the right, above the corner of Cock Lane, is the:

23. **Fat Boy** (or Golden Boy), erected by the City of London together with a plaque that reads: "This boy is in memory put up for the late Fire of London, occasion'd by the sin of gluttony 1666." Popular myth holds that the Great Fire was God's way of punishing overindulgent Londoners.

Continue 1 block to the end of Giltspur Street. Note on the right the **Church of the Holy Sepulchre.** Founded in 1137 just outside the City wall's Northern Gate, this was the departure point for the knights of the Crusades. It was named after the Holy Sepulchre Church in Jerusalem, the Crusaders' destination. The present building dates from 1450.

At the intersection of Giltspur and Newgate streets is the:

☕ **Take a Break**   **Viaduct Tavern,** 126 Newgate St.
(☎ **0171/606-8476**). Built in 1875, this is the City
of London's only remaining example of a late 19th-century
Gin Palace. The pub's copper ceiling and painted oils on
canvas were intended to attract customers from their ordinary dwellings to this spectacular "palace." When the pub
was refurbished in 1994, one of its original mirrors was
found, and you can see it along the staircase leading to the
rest rooms. In addition to Tetley and Pedigree bitters, the
pub offers "guest" ales that change weekly. You can order
toasted sandwiches, sausages, baked potatoes, and the like.

Directly across from the pub is the:

24. **Old Bailey Courthouse.** Known officially as the Central
Criminal Court, the world-famous Old Bailey (where John
Mortimer's famous character, barrister Horace Rumpole,
had many a legal skirmish) is named after the street on which
it stands. The building occupies the site of the former
Newgate Prison, which was demolished in 1902. Inside you
can witness trials, complete with judges in wigs and flow-
ing robes. The courtrooms are open to the public Monday
to Friday from 10am to 1pm and 2 to 4pm. Be warned that
cameras and bags aren't allowed in the building. The entrance to the public galleries are via Warwick Passage about
1 block down Old Bailey on your left.

Leave the Old Bailey from the same doors you entered
and turn left onto Old Bailey. After 1 block, turn left onto
Ludgate Hill, cross Ave Maria Lane (named for the many
religious processions held there in the Middle Ages), and
continue half a block to:

25. **St. Paul's Cathedral** (☎ **0171/248-2705**), where Prince
Charles and the late Princess Diana wed. Dedicated to the
patron saint of the City of London, St. Paul's is the masterpiece of architect Sir Christopher Wren. Wren is buried in
the cathedral's crypt; his tomb bears the Latin inscription
"Lector, si monumentum requiris, circumspice" ("Reader,
if you seek his monument, look around you").

To reach St. Paul's Underground Station, exit the cathedral, continue along St. Paul's Churchyard, turn left at New
Change, and continue until reaching Cheapside.

Dickens's London

Start: Holborn Underground Station.

Finish: Holborn Underground Station.

Time: 2½ hours.

Best Time: Monday to Friday from 1 to 4:30pm, when all the interiors on the tour are open.

Worst Time: Weekends (when much of the route is closed to the general public).

Charles Dickens was born in Portsmouth, England, on February 7, 1812. His family moved to London when he was 10, and within 2 years his life was thrown into turmoil when his father, John, was imprisoned for debt. Charles found work at Warrens Blacking Warehouse, a boot-polish maker, and entered the most miserable time of his childhood. Exactly how long he spent at Warrens is uncertain, but to the young Dickens it must've seemed like an eternity. This period was to have a profound influence on him both artistically and personally.

Dickens lived much of his life in London, and despite (or because of) his profound love/hate relationship with the city, his best works were written here. He loved to wander the streets for hours, day or night, and his novels often read like Victorian walking tours, packed with telling details. Everything he saw registered in his photographic memory—from the sights and smells of his childhood to the faces and personalities of the people he met in London's poorest parts when he was an adult.

Although you won't see the deplorable conditions that prevailed in Dickens's time (overcrowded alleys, grimy buildings, coal pollution), you will discover unexpected spots of beauty, hidden passages, and courtyards that Dickens knew and loved.

• • • • • • • • • • • • • • • • •

Exit Holborn Underground Station, turn left onto Kingsway, and then make the third left into Remnant Street. One block ahead is:

1. **Lincoln's Inn Fields,** London's largest square. Once these fields were farmland belonging to the duchess of Portsmouth, and Dickens knew them well and featured them in his novel *Barnaby Rudge.*

   By keeping to the left side of Lincoln's Inn Fields you'll arrive at:

2. **Sir John Soane's House,** 11 Lincoln's Inn Fields (☎ 0171/405-2107), open Tuesday to Saturday from 10am to 5pm. Sir John Soane, the architect of the Bank of England and 10 Downing St., lived in this house from 1792 until his death in 1837. It was left to the nation and today calls itself a "museum." This, though, is a misleading term, for it's a personal collection with paintings and exhibits arranged in the manner of Soane's own choosing. Of particular interest from a "Dickensian" point of view are the originals of William Hogarth's *The Rake's Progress* and *Election Campaign.* Admission is free.

   Hogarth was an astute observer of and commentator on the 18th-century social scene, his eye every bit as keen as Dickens's for depicting London's low life, albeit of a different century. He was a favorite artist of the young Dickens, whose style was greatly influenced by the narrative style of Hogarth's works.

Dickens's London

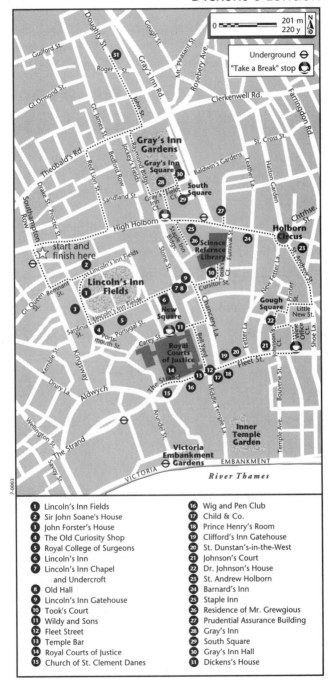

0	201 m
	220 y

Underground ⊖

"Take a Break" stop

1. Lincoln's Inn Fields
2. Sir John Soane's House
3. John Forster's House
4. The Old Curiosity Shop
5. Royal College of Surgeons
6. Lincoln's Inn
7. Lincoln's Inn Chapel and Undercroft
8. Old Hall
9. Lincoln's Inn Gatehouse
10. Took's Court
11. Wildy and Sons
12. Fleet Street
13. Temple Bar
14. Royal Courts of Justice
15. Church of St. Clement Danes
16. Wig and Pen Club
17. Child & Co.
18. Prince Henry's Room
19. Clifford's Inn Gatehouse
20. St. Dunstan's-in-the-West
21. Johnson's Court
22. Dr. Johnson's House
23. St. Andrew Holborn
24. Barnard's Inn
25. Staple Inn
26. Residence of Mr. Grewgious
27. Prudential Assurance Building
28. Gray's Inn
29. South Square
30. Gray's Inn Hall
31. Dickens's House

Exit the museum and retrace your footsteps counter-clockwise around the square until you arrive at:

3. **John Forster's House,** 58 Lincoln's Inn Fields. Constructed in 1730, the house was divided in two in the 1790s, when the ornate porch was added. John Forster, a lawyer as well as the book and drama editor of *The Examiner,* lived here from 1834 to 1856. One of Dickens's best friends and a trusted confidant, he often accompanied Dickens on rambunctious rambles around the city. They often discussed work, and Dickens relied on Forster for business and creative advice. Forster went on to become Dickens's primary biographer.

In *Bleak House,* Dickens modeled the home of Mr. Tulkinghorn, a sinister lawyer, on this house. He describes it as "a large house, formerly a house of state . . . let off in chambers now; and in those shrunken fragments of greatness lawyers lie like maggots in nuts."

On December 2, 1844, in an upstairs room, Dickens gave a private reading from his sentimental Christmas novel *The Chimes.* The select gathering of literary figures included Wilkie Collins, author of *The Woman in White.* The reading proved such a success that Dickens decided to repeat it 3 days later. From these informal gatherings, Dickens went on to public readings that became so popular he continued them all over Britain and later took them to America. These exhausting trips may have contributed to his premature death at 58 in 1870.

Walk straight out of Lincoln's Inn Fields, onto Portsmouth Street. A few yards down on the left is:

4. **The Old Curiosity Shop,** 13–14 Portsmouth St. Predecessors of today's variety stores, curiosity shops sold such items as quill pens, paper, and other necessities and novelties. Constructed in 1567 from the wood of dismantled ships, this building first served as two farm laborers' cottages on land owned by the duchess of Portsmouth. It was remodeled as one building in the 18th century.

In Dickens's day, this store was owned by a bookbinder named Tessyman. It's believed that Tessyman's granddaughter inspired Dickens to create the child heroine Little Nell for *The Old Curiosity Shop.* Although Dickens wrote that the actual shop he "immortalized" was demolished in his lifetime, he would certainly have been familiar with this building.

Return to Lincoln's Inn Fields and turn right, continuing counterclockwise around the square. The wonderful neoclassical building on your right is the:

5. **Royal College of Surgeons,** 35 Lincoln's Inn Fields. This impressive building from the 1830s was designed by Charles Barry, who also designed the Houses of Parliament. Dickens refers to it in *Bleak House,* when Mr. Boythorn comments that the lawyers of Lincoln's Inn should have their "necks rung and their skulls arranged in Surgeons Hall, for the contemplation of the whole profession, in order that its younger members might understand from actual measurement in early life, how thick skulls may become!"

Exit Lincoln's Inn Fields through the stone gate just ahead and enter:

6. **Lincoln's Inn.** This compound is home to one of London's four Inns of Court, societies to which all aspiring and practicing barristers belong. These institutions, dating back to the 14th century, were called "inns" because they provided room and board for their students. Today, tradition still requires legal apprentices to dine with their fraternity 24 times before they're admitted to the bar. Practicing barristers must continue to dine with the society at least three times during each law term in order to maintain their membership. Unlike solicitors, who prepare the briefs for the cases, barristers (wearing wigs and robes) have a monopoly on pleading in the higher courts.

As you pass through the gates, look at the building immediately to your left. This is **Lincoln's Inn New Hall,** the barristers' dining hall, built in 1843. On the right is **New Square,** an office complex of barristers' chambers dating from the 1620s.

Walk under the archway directly ahead, into the Old Courtyard. The building on your left is:

7. **Lincoln's Inn Chapel and Undercroft.** This chapel was designed by Inigo Jones, one of London's most famous architects. In 1619, the building's foundation stone was laid by the renowned metaphysical poet/preacher John Donne,

who also presided over the chapel's consecration on Ascension Day 1623. The undercroft (covered cloisterlike walkway) was intended to be a place where students could "walk and talk and confer for their learning," as well as a private spot where barristers could meet their clients. There are several tombstones along the undercroft, including that of John Thurloe, secretary of state under Oliver Cromwell (Lord Protector, 1653–58).

The building behind you and to your right is the:

8. **Old Hall,** Lincoln's Inn, an aptly named building from the second half of the 15th century. From 1737 to 1875, the Hall housed the High Court of Chancery, England's court of finance and property, when the main court in Westminster Hall was on holiday. Dickens disliked the Court of Chancery, since he had worked there as a court reporter. The Old Hall and the Court of Chancery were targeted by Dickens's vitriolic pen in *Bleak House,* which told of the trial of *Jarndyce* v. *Jarndyce,* a case that had begun so long ago that no one could remember what it was about:

"This is the Court of Chancery; which has its decaying houses and its blighted lands in every shire; which has its worn-out lunatic in every madhouse, and its dead in every churchyard; which has its ruined suitor, with his slipshod heels and threadbare dress, borrowing and begging through the round of every man's acquaintance; which gives to monied might the means abundantly of wearying out the right; which so exhausts finances, patience, courage, hope; so overthrows the brain and breaks the heart; that there is not an honourable man among its practitioners who would not give—who does not often give—the warning, 'Suffer any wrong that can be done you, rather than come here!'"

Visitors aren't usually allowed into the Old Hall, but if the doors are open (which often happens), it can't hurt to try to look in.

Now walk straight across the courtyard through:

9. **Lincoln's Inn Gatehouse,** a security gate built between 1517 and 1521 by Sir Thomas Lovell, the son of Henry VIII's chancellor. Above the doors you can see Lovell's coat of arms, together with those of Henry VIII and the earl of Lincoln, this area's former landowner. According to biographer John

Forster, when Dickens was a young boy, he was walking through this gate when "a big blackguard fellow walked up to me, doffed my cap and said 'hulloa soldier,' which I could not stand so I at once struck him and he then hit me in the eye."

Exit right through the gatehouse, cross over Chancery Lane, and make the first left into Cursitor Street. Continue for 1 block and turn left into:

10. **Took's Court.** In *Bleak House,* Dickens renamed this Cook's Court, and it's here that Mr. Snagsby, Law Stationer, "pursues his lawful calling. . . . In the shade of Cook's Court, at most times a shady place, Mr. Snagsby had dealt in all sorts of blank forms of legal process." Today this thin street still evokes an air of shadiness, and two 18th-century houses, one actually called "Dickens House," lend it a dignified air.

Retrace your footsteps to Chancery Lane and turn left. Continue ahead for 2 blocks and turn right into Carey Street. Two blocks along, turn right through Lincoln's Inn Gatehouse, where immediately on your right is:

11. **Wildy and Sons,** Lincoln's Inn Archway, Carey Street (☎ 0171/242-5778), which has the distinction of being the oldest legal bookseller in London, having traded since 1798. You'll find new and secondhand law books, as well as collectible legal prints like *The Law Suit,* a caricature of two farmers fighting over a cow—one pulls on the horns and the other pulls on the tail, while between them sits the lawyer, milking the cow. The shop is open Monday to Friday from 8:45am to 5:15pm.

Return to Carey Street and continue along until you arrive at the:

Take a Break **Seven Stars,** Carey Street (☎ 0171/242-8521), one of London's smallest pubs. This atmospheric place dates back to 1602 and is named for the seven provinces of the Netherlands. Prints of Dickensian characters adorn the walls, and the chat is of legal matters and gossip, since the pub is a favored haunt of lawyers and journalists enjoying a break from the rigors of the **Royal Courts of Justice** opposite. Beers served include Directors and Courage Best, and the food consists of sandwiches and stews.

Exit the pub and cross the street, turning left along Carey Street. Take the first turning right into Bell Yard and then make a right at the end onto:

12. **Fleet Street,** named for a nearby river (now covered over) that flows from Hampstead. This street is synonymous with journalism and once accommodated the printing facilities and offices of most London newspapers (as well as the blood-thirsty Sweeney Todd). Since the *Daily Telegraph* and *Daily Express* moved from their respective buildings several years ago, no newspapers are headquartered here now. Dickens knew this area intimately and often walked along this street throughout his lifetime.

Continue on for 1 block and you'll notice in the center of the street a monument called:

13. **Temple Bar.** This 20-foot-high obelisk marks the boundary between the City of London (which you're about to leave) and Westminster. In *Bleak House,* Dickens refers to "that leaden-headed, old obstruction, appropriate ornament for the threshold of a leaden-headed old corporation: Temple Bar." As you pass the obelisk, notice that Fleet Street ends and the road changes name to The Strand.

The buildings on your right are the:

14. **Royal Courts of Justice,** designed and built by architect George Street between 1872 and 1882. This spectacular Gothic building was erected with about 35 million bricks and boasts more than 1,000 rooms and more than 3½ miles of corridors. Stand directly outside the main entrance and look up to see a sculpture of Christ, flanked by statues of King Solomon (left) and King Alfred (right).

Inside the main hall of this high English court is a small exhibit of the official garments worn by judges and barristers. You're free to walk around the building and glance into the courtrooms. Here and in the halls you can see the judges dressed in ermine-trimmed robes and full-bottomed wigs. Cameras aren't allowed inside, but close to the courts is a newsstand that will hold your camera (for a small fee) while you're inside.

Cross over the pedestrian crossing outside the Royal Courts. To your right is the:

15. **Church of St. Clement Danes.** Inside is a memorial to members of the U.S. Air Force who were stationed in England during World War II.

     Turn left on the opposite side and backtrack along The Strand. Just past the next crossing, you'll come to the:

16. **Wig and Pen Club,** 229–230 The Strand (☎ **0171/ 583-7255**). Begun in 1625, this famous fraternity is London's most exclusive club for lawyers and journalists. There are several private bars, but the basement restaurant is open to the public. You can get a temporary membership in order to be able to drink at the bar adjoining the restaurant.

     Continue walking along The Strand; just beyond Temple Bar on the right is:

17. **Child & Co.,** 1 Fleet St., a private bank started by Francis Child in 1673. Child's bank was the model for Tellson's Bank in Dickens's *A Tale of Two Cities.*

     Continue along Fleet Street and to the right of the traffic lights is:

18. **Prince Henry's Room,** 17 Fleet St. (no phone), contained in a fantastically preserved building from 1610; it's one of the few remaining wooden structures that survived London's Great Fire of 1666.

     First an inn called the Princes Arms, the building later housed Mrs. Salmon's Waxworks, a kind of early Madame Tussaud's that became a favorite haunt of the young Dickens. In *David Copperfield,* Dickens's hero goes "to see some perspiring wax works in Fleet Street" and mocks the funny-looking, sweating figures. Today Prince Henry's Room is a museum focusing on 17th-century diarist Samuel Pepys (for more on Pepys, see Stop 3 in Walking Tour 3), open Monday to Saturday from 11am to 2pm; admission is free.

     The staircase to the left of the front gates takes you up to the small yet beautifully constructed room. One set of feathers appears on the ceiling, together with Prince Henry's initials. Henry was the eldest son of James I; his untimely death at the age of 18 led to his brother's inheriting the throne as Charles I.

Cross Fleet Street via the pedestrian crossing, turn right, and, just past Chancery Lane, turn left into the narrow alleyway called Clifford's Inn Passage. At the end of the alley is the 17th-century:

19. **Clifford's Inn Gatehouse,** all that remains of the Old Inn, which was a prep school for aspiring attorneys from the 15th through the 18th century. In Dickens's *Little Dorrit,* Little Dorrit's brother, Tip, found "a stool and twelve shillings a week in the office of the attorney in Clifford's Inn and here languished for six months."

This was a rather unpleasant place in Dickens's day. In *Our Mutual Friend,* John Rokesmith, a principal character, meets Mr. Boffin on the street and says, "'Would you object to turn aside into this place—I think it is called Clifford's Inn—where we can hear one another better than in the roaring street?' Mr. Boffin glanced into the mouldy little plantation, or cat-preserve, of Clifford's Inn as it was that day. . . . Sparrows were there, dry rot and wet rot were there but it was not otherwise a suggestive spot."

Return to Fleet Street and turn left; two doors along is:

20. **St. Dunstan's-in-the-West,** Fleet Street, an octagonal church. The large clock on the tower was installed by the congregation to express its thanks that the building was spared from the Great Fire. However, the original church was totally replaced from 1829 to 1833. The present building is an excellent early example of Gothic Revival architecture. The clock dates to 1671; its two giant clubs still strike a reverberating bell every 15 minutes. This was the first clock in London with a double face and with minutes marked on its dial. Dickens mentioned the clock in both *Barnaby Rudge* and *David Copperfield.*

Once inside the church, turn right; on the wall of the third shrine is a **memorial** to a "famed swordsman" and to an "honest solicitor." In the opposite corner is a beautiful **icon screen** brought here from Antim Monastery in Bucharest.

Exit the church, turn left, and continue along Fleet Street. Two doors away (just after no. 185), turn into **Hen and Chickens Court,** where you'll see an extremely Dickensian inner court. It was here, in the Victorian melodrama, that the fictitious shop of Sweeney Todd, the Demon Barber of

Fleet Street, was located. Return to Fleet Street and cross Fetter Lane. Just past the bus stop, on your left, is:

21. **Johnson's Court.** Although nothing from Dickens's day survives on this street, the writer's career began here. This was once the address of *Monthly Magazine*'s office. John Forster wrote that Dickens, "stealthily one evening at twilight," dropped off, "with fear and trembling," an article that *Monthly Magazine* accepted. It became his first published piece. This, as well as other early works by Dickens, was published under the pseudonym "Boz," his younger brother's nickname.

Continue 2 blocks farther along Fleet Street and turn left into Wine Office Court. A few yards up on the right is:

Take a Break **Ye Olde Cheshire Cheese,** Wine Office Court, 145 Fleet St. (☎ **0171/353-6170**), one of the city's oldest pubs and one of Dickens's favorite watering holes. The vaulted cellar may have been part of the Old Whitefriars Monastery that once occupied this site. There has been a tavern here since the 1590s. After it burned down in the Great Fire, Ye Olde Cheshire Cheese was quickly rebuilt, thus becoming the first pub to reopen after the fire. Downstairs, you can still see charred wooden beams that date back to that event.

Dickens's regular table, mentioned in *A Tale of Two Cities,* was to the right of the fireplace, opposite the bar in the ground-floor room.

Earlier in this century the pub gained an additional measure of fame thanks to its foul-mouthed mascot, Polly the parrot. On Armistice Day 1918, the bird imitated the popping of a champagne cork 400 times and then fainted. Throughout the 1920s Polly was renowned for her ability to swear in several languages. Her 1926 death was announced on the BBC World Service, and the *London Times* carried her obituary under the headline "International Expert in Profanity Dies." You can find Polly, now stuffed and mounted and looking somewhat bedraggled, on a window ledge in the back bar.

Continue through Wine Office Court, bear left at the tree, and walk half a block into Gough (*"Goff"*) Square to:

22. **Dr. Johnson's House,** 17 Gough Sq. (☎ 0171/353-3745). A significant literary scholar and critic, Samuel Johnson (1709–84) lived and worked here, compiling the world's first English-language dictionary. He lived quite humbly: When artist Joshua Reynolds visited Dr. Johnson's long attic, he observed that "besides his books, all covered with dust, there was an old crazy meal table, and still worse, an older elbow chair having only three legs." Johnson's house is now a museum of memorabilia; his original dictionary is on display. It's open Monday to Saturday from 11am to 5pm. Admission is charged.

Exit Gough Square through the passage opposite Dr. Johnson's House. Turn left onto Gunpowder Square, then head straight to Printer Street. Turn right onto Little New Street and left onto Shoe Lane, which after 2 blocks becomes St. Andrew Street. Continue 250 yards ahead to Holborn Circus. The **statue** in the center of the road is of Queen Victoria's consort, Prince Albert. He's raising his hat to the City of London, an act that has led this to be dubbed "London's politest statue." On the corner to your right is:

23. **St. Andrew Holborn,** Holborn Circus, the largest Sir Christopher Wren–designed parish church. On his death in 1348, a local merchant, John Thane, willed all his houses and shops to this church; his bequest provides for the church's upkeep to this day. Dickens mentioned St. Andrew in *Oliver Twist:* The burglar Bill Sykes looks up at the clock tower and says to Oliver, "Hard upon seven! You must step out." The two left from here and robbed a house.

There has been a succession of churches on this site since the year 951. The present building, which was damaged by air raids during World War II, was restored in 1961.

Turn left onto Holborn and walk 1 block. Just after the Midland Bank, you'll see the entrance to:

24. **Barnard's Inn,** a former prep school for students of the Inns of Court. It's confusing that so many buildings are called "inns," and apparently Dickens thought so too. In *Great Expectations,* the protagonist, Pip, says of Barnard's, "I had supposed that establishment to be a hotel kept by Mr. Barnard. Whereas I now found Barnard to be a

disembodied spirit, or a fiction, and his inn the dingiest collection of shabby buildings ever squeezed together in a rank corner as a club for Tom-cats."

One block ahead on Holborn, on the left, is:

25. **Staple Inn,** headquarters of the Institute of Actuaries. The inn, whose timber front dates from 1576, is London's last existing example of domestic architecture from Shakespeare's day. It was originally a hostel for wool staplers, or brokers, and thus the name. Walk through the gates, where a sign on your left warns: "The porter has orders to prevent old clothes men and others from calling 'articles for sale'"—in other words, "No soliciting."

Once inside, you'll find yourself in one of a few tranquil oases that even Dickens liked. As he wrote in *The Mystery of Edwin Drood:* "Behind the most ancient part of Holborn, London, where certain gabled houses some centuries of age still stand looking on the public way . . . is a little nook called Staple Inn. It is one of those nooks the turning into which out of the clashing streets, imparts to the relieved pedestrian the sensation of having put cotton in his ears and velvet soles on his boots." Pause and consider just how little this place has changed since Dickens wrote those sentences.

Cross the cobblestone courtyard, walk through the covered passageway, and look at the building immediately on your left. This is the:

26. **Residence of Mr. Grewgious,** the kindly lawyer in *The Mystery of Edwin Drood.* A stone above the door bears the inscription "PJT 1747." In the novel, Dickens wondered why Grewgious wasn't curious about what PJT might stand for, other than "perhaps John Thomas" or "probably Joe Tyler." In fact, the initials are those of the inn's then-president, John Thompson.

Turn right into the unmarked walkway, climb the steps, and turn right onto Staple Inn Buildings (a road). At the end, find the entrance to Chancery Lane Underground Station. Use this underpass to cross under Holborn; once past the telephones, take the exit on your right through the tunnel. Go up the stairs and walk half a block to London's last great example of Gothic Revival, the:

27. **Prudential Assurance Building.** This large structure of red brick and terra-cotta was designed by Alfred Waterhouse in 1879. Enter through the gates opposite the bus stop and cross to the other side; in a small grotto you'll see a bust of Charles Dickens. The Prudential Building stands on the site of Furnivals Inn, where Dickens lived from 1834 to 1837. During this time he began writing *The Pickwick Papers,* the work that secured his literary fame.

Return to Holborn and turn right. Cross Gray's Inn Road and continue along Holborn until you reach the:

☕ **Take a Break** **Citte of York Pub,** 22–23 High Holborn (☎ 0171/242-7670). Even though it's one of the largest pubs around, this grand Victorian-style tavern offers unparalleled intimacy in cozy cubicles. Once popular with lawyers who came here to speak confidentially with clients, the pub now draws office workers and other savvy patrons. In the cellar is a second bar.

Exit the pub and immediately turn left down a small alley to:

28. **Gray's Inn,** another of London's four Inns of Court and one that certainly didn't impress Dickens. In *The Uncommercial Traveller,* he wrote: "Indeed, I look upon Gray's Inn generally as one of the most depressing institutions in brick and mortar known to the children of men."

The passageway opens up into a part of the inn called:

29. **South Square.** In 1828, when Dickens was 16, he worked here as a clerk for the law firm Ellis and Blackmore (1 South Sq.). The mischievous author-to-be used to drop small stones from the upstairs windows onto the heads of unsuspecting lawyers. Dickens learned shorthand here because his father felt that the training would enable him to become a reporter at Doctors Commons (the College of Advocates and Doctors of Law). Although Dickens's career goals changed, the shorthand he learned probably led to his phonetic style of writing. If you look inside the front entrance of **no. 1,** you'll see a portrait of Dickens as a young man.

The black **statue** on the far side of the lawn is of Sir Francis Bacon, Lord Chancellor of England under Elizabeth I. The statue was erected in 1912 and shows

Bacon wearing his official robes. He was a writer, philosopher, and influential scientific theorist, and his best-known work is his *Essays,* remarkable for their pithy, epigrammatic style.

The churchlike building at the far side of the square is:

30. **Gray's Inn Hall.** Built in 1556, the hall hosted the first performance of Shakespeare's *Comedy of Errors* in 1594. This square is mentioned in many of Dickens's novels. From *The Pickwick Papers:* "Clerk after clerk hastened into the square by one or other of the entrances, and looking up at the hall clock accelerated or decreased his rate of walking according to the time at which his office hours nominally commenced."

Exit South Square on the road running along the left side of Gray's Inn Hall and take the first left onto the path running under the buildings. Pass the gardens and take the first right onto Gray's Inn Place (the sign reads "To Raymond Buildings"). Turn right onto Theobald's Road, then take the first left onto John Street, which becomes Doughty Street. About 5 blocks ahead, on your right, is:

31. **Dickens's House,** 48 Doughty St. (☎ 0171/405-2127), the author's only surviving London home. He moved here in 1837, before he was well known. While living here, Dickens finished *The Pickwick Papers,* as well as *Oliver Twist* and *Nicholas Nickleby,* and started work on *Barnaby Rudge.* By the time he left this house in 1839, he was world famous. You can see the author's letters, furniture, and first editions in glass display cases, adjacent to rooms that've been restored. The house is open Monday to Saturday from 10am to 5pm; there's an admission charge.

Return to Theobald's Road and turn right. Four blocks along, turn left into Red Lion Street and at the end turn right onto High Holborn. Keep to the left side for 3 blocks to arrive back at the Holborn Underground Station.

A Historic Pub Walk

Start: Embankment Underground Station.

Finish: Covent Garden Underground Station.

Time: 2½ hours, including pauses to quench your thirst.

Best Time: During pub hours: Monday to Saturday from 11am to 11pm and Sunday from noon to 10:30pm. If you take your walk around lunch time, you can sample traditional "pub grub." After 5pm or around sunset is a good time to drink with the locals.

Worst Time: Late at night, when the streets are dark, and on Sunday, when many sights are closed.

There's nothing more British than a pub. The public house is exactly that—the British public's place to meet, exchange stories, tell jokes, grab a quick bite, and drink. Many efforts have been made to create something resembling a pub outside Britain, but they just don't capture the unique feel of the real McCoy. Pubs are almost as old as England itself. In the 12th century, William Fitzstephen (secretary to Thomas à Becket) noted that London was cursed by two plagues: fire and drink. An occasional afternoon or, more often, evening spent in a pub is part of British social life. And on Sunday afternoon, entire families often go to the pub for lunch. (Note, however, that children under 14 aren't allowed in pubs at all, and no one under 18 may legally be served alcohol.)

Beer is the principal drink sold in pubs, available in imperial half-pints and pints (20% larger than U.S. measures). The choice is usually between lager and bitter, and the locals usually prefer the latter. Many pubs serve particularly good "real" ales, which can be distinguished at the bar by hand pumps that the barkeeps must "pull." Real ales are natural "live" beers that've been allowed to ferment in the cask. Unlike lagers, English ales are served at room temperature and may take some getting used to. For an unusual and tasty alternative, try cider, a flavorful fermented apple juice that's so good you'll hardly notice the alcohol—until later.

As a rule, there's no table service in pubs; you order drinks and food at the bar and carry everything to your table. Tipping isn't customary; it should be reserved for exemplary service.

Pubs used to be required to close in the afternoons, but a 1988 change in the law—which most people toasted—now allows them to stay open on Monday to Saturday from 11am to 11pm; in 1995 they were also allowed to open on Sunday from noon to 10:30pm. Not all pubs choose to take advantage of this new freedom, however; some still close daily between 3 and 7pm.

Carpeted floors, etched glass, and carved-wood bars are the hallmarks of most pubs. But each one looks different, and each has its own special atmosphere and clientele. Greater London's 7,000-plus pubs mean that you'll never have to walk more than a couple of blocks to find one, and part of the enjoyment of "pubbing" is discovering a special one on your own. This tour will take you to some of the most famous and some of the least known watering holes in the city—an excellent cross-section of taverns united by their historic uniqueness. Cheers!

• • • • • • • • • • • • • • •

Take the left exit from Embankment Underground Station and walk up Villiers Street. Don't walk too far, though. The first brown wooden door on your right is the entrance to:

1. **Gordon's,** 47 Villiers St. (☎ **0171/930-1408**). Though not a pub, this is the most atmospheric and eccentric wine bar that you'll ever visit. Wine bars are a relatively recent phenomenon in London, offering an excellent alternative to the traditional pub. Most have a good selection by the glass or the bottle, and food is almost always served. The menus tend to have a continental emphasis, with standards and prices that are higher than at most pubs. You don't have to eat, however; in fact, a bottle of the house wine shared among two or three people may be less expensive than visiting a pub.

   At Gordon's, framed yellowed newspapers adorn the walls; model Spitfires, covered in dust, hang from the ceiling; and rickety tables crowd the floor. The candlelit drinking room features intimately low-vaulted ceilings. Gordon's unusual decor and atmosphere make it an important stop on this tour. It's not open on Saturday or Sunday.

   Leaving Gordon's, turn left onto Villiers Street and immediately left again down the steps to Watergate Walk. Stroll along the pathway until, half a block ahead on your right, you come to the:

2. **Duke of Buckingham's watergate.** Before the 1862 construction of the Victoria Embankment (which keeps the Thames in check), this stone gateway marked the river's high-tide line and protected the duke's mansion (which once stood behind it). The inscription on top of the gate reads "Fidei Coticula Crux" ("The cross is the touchstone of faith")—the duke's family motto. After the mansion was demolished in 1675, the grounds were turned into a public park. These are the gardens that George Orwell wrote about in *Down and Out in Paris and London* and the place where Orwell slept while living as a vagrant in the 1930s.

   With your back to the watergate, climb the flight of stone steps, walk through the iron gate, and enter Buckingham Street. On your left is:

3. **14 Buckingham St.,** the former home of Samuel Pepys (1633–1703). Despite a long and distinguished career as an official in naval affairs, Pepys is best remembered for the detailed diary he kept from 1660 to 1669. Thanks to this we know more about him than about any other person of

A Historic Pub Walk

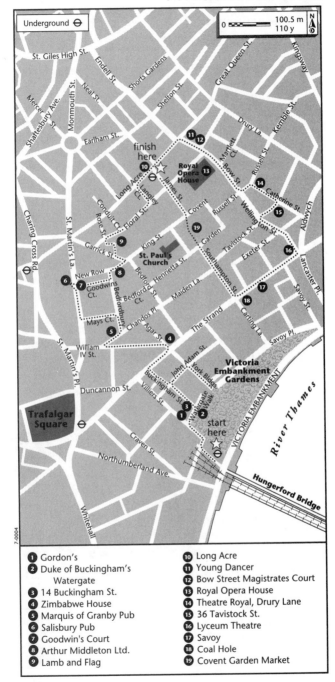

1. Gordon's
2. Duke of Buckingham's Watergate
3. 14 Buckingham St.
4. Zimbabwe House
5. Marquis of Granby Pub
6. Salisbury Pub
7. Goodwin's Court
8. Arthur Middleton Ltd.
9. Lamb and Flag
10. Long Acre
11. Young Dancer
12. Bow Street Magistrates Court
13. Royal Opera House
14. Theatre Royal, Drury Lane
15. 36 Tavistock St.
16. Lyceum Theatre
17. Savoy
18. Coal Hole
19. Covent Garden Market

his time. He concealed the contents of his diary from his wife by using his own personal code—a complex mix of foreign and invented words. Pepys's diary is not only an important history of the events and manners of his day but also a fascinating psychological study of Pepys himself. After he had spent the evening with an actress and was back home, he wrote that his wife pulled aside the bed curtain and with red-hot tongs "made as if she did design to pinch me with them." Most of Pepys's entries were written at night by candlelight, a practice that eventually ruined his eyesight. The diarist moved from this house in 1701, 2 years before his death.

This area (encompassing the site of Pepys's house) was developed in the late 18th century as a housing project called **Adelphi.** It was initiated by three brothers—John, Robert, and James Adam (*Adelphoi* is Greek for brothers)—and financed by a lottery with the approval of an Act of Parliament. The houses were built on arches, vaults, and subterranean streets, so that they'd rise above the mud of the Thames. Few of these houses now remain, but if you turn right on John Adam Street, right again on York Buildings, and then left into the narrow York Way, you can explore one of these vaults. Within their confines, in years past, "the most abandoned characters have often passed the night, nestling upon foul straw; and many a street thief escaped from his pursuers in these dismal haunts." One of the most attractive of the remaining homes belonged to Robert Adam—at **7 Adam St.** (which you can see from John Adam St. as you turn into York Buildings).

Return to John Adam Street and turn left and then right at Buckingham Street. Climb the steps of the National Westminster Bank and walk through Buckingham Arcade to The Strand. Cross at the crosswalk and turn right on The Strand; at the corner of Agar Street look across at:

4. **Zimbabwe House,** the home of the Zimbabwe High Commission. Look up at the second-story windows, between which stand nude statues depicting the Ages of Man. The figures caused such an outcry when they were unveiled by sculptor Jacob Epstein in 1908 that the windows of the building across the street were replaced with frosted glass to obscure the view. After the Southern Rhodesian High

Commission moved into the building in the 1930s, one of the statue's "private" parts broke off and almost struck a pedestrian below. Orders were given to "remove the protruding parts" of the statues, which is why none of them now has a "head."

Turn sharply left onto William IV Street, then right into Chandos Place. On the next corner is the:

5. **Marquis of Granby Pub,** 51 Chandos Place (☎ 0171/836-7657). This tavern dates from the reign of Charles II, when it was known as the Hole in the Wall and run by an ex-mistress of the second duke of Buckingham. In the 19th century, Claude Duval, one of England's most notorious robbers and a consummate ladies' man, was arrested while drinking here. After his trial and execution, Duval was buried under a tombstone that reads:

Here lies Duval.
Reader: if male thou art, look to thy purse
If female, to thy heart.

The pub was renamed in the late 18th century in honor of Gen. John Manners, the marquis of Granby, who led the English army in 1759 at the Battle of Minden during the Seven Years' War that resulted in a victory over the French. Today, the cheerful English-inn atmosphere makes this place popular with actors and workers from the nearby theaters. The pub serves several cask-conditioned "real" ales, a monthly guest beer, and a traditional menu (until 9pm). It's especially busy at lunch time.

Exit the pub and turn left onto Bedfordbury, past the stage doors of London Coliseum, home of the English National Opera.

One block ahead, turn left onto Mays Court, then right onto St. Martin's Lane. Diagonally across the street from the Lumiere Cinema on your left is the:

6. **Salisbury Pub,** 90 St. Martin's Lane (☎ 0171/836-5863). Formerly known as the Coach and Horses and later as Ben Caunts's Head, this 1852 tavern gained fame for the bare-knuckle prize fights that used to take place here. Beautifully preserved, the pub's magnificent marble fittings, cut-glass mirrors, brass statuettes, plush seats, and art nouveau

decor make it one of the most attractive in London. The quintessential theater pub, the Salisbury touts itself as the "archetype of actors' pubs, and as much a part of the world of the stage as greasepaint."

As you leave the Salisbury, cross St. Martin's Lane; almost directly ahead, climb the two steps at 55–56 St. Martin's Lane to enter:

7. **Goodwin's Court,** an almost secret, wonderfully preserved 18th-century street. At night, the bucolic gas lamp–lit court looks like a flawless Hollywood set. It's pure magic.

Walk through Goodwin's Court and turn left on Bedfordbury. On the corner of New Row is:

8. **Arthur Middleton Ltd.,** 12 New Row, purveyors of antique scientific tools and instruments. Take a look inside; you might find centuries-old telescopes, weather data devices, and surgical instruments. The window displays are usually rather interesting as well.

Turn right onto New Row, left onto Garrick Street, and then immediately right onto Rose Street to the:

9. **Lamb and Flag,** 33 Rose St. (☎ 0171/497-9504). Built in 1623, this wood-frame structure is remarkable because it survived the Great Fire of 1666 (such structures proved highly flammable). A favorite haunt of Charles Dickens, this pub was once known as the "Bucket of Blood" because of the prize fights held here for betting customers. Poet John Dryden (1631–1700) was attacked and beaten in the side alley by thugs probably hired by the earl of Rochester, who was unhappy about a vicious lampoon by Dryden. The anniversary of the December 16 attack is marked each year when the Lamb and Flag holds a festive Dryden Night.

Leave the pub by the side exit, turn left down the narrow wood-lined alley called Lazenby Court and turn right onto upscale Floral Street. After about 300 yards, turn left onto Langley Court, then right onto:

10. **Long Acre,** Covent Garden's main thoroughfare and a popular shopping street. Built on a sloping hill, Long Acre connects Covent Garden with Leicester Square. At night, especially on weekends, this is one of the busiest streets in London.

Walk about 3 blocks (along which you'll find great window shopping), pass the Covent Garden Underground Station, turn right onto Bow Street, and walk 1 block to see:

11. **Young Dancer,** a beautiful statue by Enzo Plazzotta (1921–81), on your left. London is packed with outdoor statues—some 1,700 at last count—but most are old memorials to even older statesmen. *Young Dancer* is one of the few examples of good modern outdoor sculpture in London. This statue honors dancers of the Royal Ballet who perform at the Royal Opera House, just across the street.

Next to the statue on the corner is the:

12. **Bow Street Magistrates Court.** Henry Fielding, author of *The History of Tom Jones,* became a Justice of the Peace in 1747 and ran his court at 4 Bow St. (now demolished). Along with his blind half brother, John, Fielding helped establish the Bow Street Runners, London's first salaried, permanent police force.

Opposite the court is the:

13. **Royal Opera House** (☎ **0171/240-1066**), home to both the Royal Opera and the Royal Ballet. Originally called the Theatre Royal Covent Garden, this is the third theater to stand on this site (the previous two were destroyed by fire). On the portico are stone carvings from the preceding theater—*The Comic Muse* by John Flaxman and *The Tragic Muse* by J. C. Rossi. These sculptors also created the frieze across the front of the building. The present theater, designed by E. M. Barry, opened in 1858.

In 1919, when the theater was still used for general events, Lowell Thomas presented a 2-hour travelogue here, introducing the British to the relatively unknown Lawrence of Arabia (the script was coauthored by the then-unknown Dale Carnegie). The audience gave the film a standing ovation, and the *Times* critic wrote that it was "a triumphant vindication of the power of moving pictures, accompanied by a spoken story, to charm the eye, entertain the spirit, and move to its very depths the soul." Soon audiences were lining up all night in the hope of getting in to see it. The only person who complained was T. E. Lawrence himself; he said that his life had become very difficult, since eager crowds began surrounding him on the street. However,

Lawrence and Thomas became good friends. Thomas was often asked for anecdotes about Lawrence, and when Thomas tried to check out one story, Lawrence laughed and said: "Use it if it suits your needs. What difference does it make if it's true? History is seldom true."

Continue 2 blocks down Bow Street, turn left onto Russell Street, and then immediately turn right onto Catherine Street to the:

14. **Theatre Royal, Drury Lane,** Catherine Street (☎ 0171/ 836-8108), one of London's oldest theaters. It was opened under a royal charter in 1663 by playwright/Poet Laureate Thomas Killigrew (believed to be the illegitimate son of Shakespeare). Killigrew also made theatrical history by hiring, in 1666, the first female actor to perform professionally on the English stage.

In 1742 David Garrick, one of the city's most famous actors, made his debut here. Five years later he became the theater's manager and staged numerous Shakespearean revivals. The theater changed hands in 1777, when it was taken over by Richard Brinsley Sheridan. Unfortunately, the building wasn't insured, and when it caught fire in 1809, all Sheridan could do was sit with a glass of port and watch the blaze, commenting that "surely a man may take a glass of wine by his own fireside." The present building, from 1812, is modeled after the Grand Théâtre at Bordeaux. Major musicals are often staged here.

Jerome Kern's *Showboat* opened here in 1929, with Paul Robeson singing the lead role. His rendition of "Ol' Man River" made him an overnight celebrity. Afterward he remarked that England seemed to be relatively free of racial prejudice. As it happened, however, a celebration was held in his honor at the Savoy Grill Room, but he was refused entrance. This embarrassing and egregious mistake even reached discussion in the House of Commons.

Guided tours of the theater are available on Monday and Tuesday at 11am and 1, 3, and 5:30pm; Wednesday and Saturday at 11am and 12:30pm; and Sunday at noon and 2 and 3:30pm. There is a charge. For reservations, call ☎ 0171/494-5091.

Continue down Catherine Street and turn right on Tavistock Street. Across the road is:

15. **36 Tavistock St.,** the former home of Thomas de Quincey
    (1785–1859), author of *Confessions of an English Opium
    Eater*. When de Quincey was a young man, he started tak-
    ing opium to numb the effects of a painful gastric disease.
    Before long he became heavily addicted and, for most of
    his life, was just barely able to support his family by writing
    newspaper and magazine articles. As an old man, he be-
    came a celebrated eccentric—alone and poverty stricken.

    Just a few steps ahead, turn left onto Wellington Street.
    Walk down the hill until you come to the:

16. **Lyceum Theatre,** built in 1771. Over the years the build-
    ing has housed theatrical performances, a circus, and (in
    1802) Madame Tussaud's first London Waxworks exhibi-
    tions. Its heyday was perhaps the late 19th century, when
    Henry Irving and Ellen Terry performed here in a number
    of Shakespearean plays. In the 1960s, when the building
    was a dance hall, John Lennon staged the first public per-
    formance of his Plastic Ono Band.

    Turn right on The Strand, cross to the south side of the
    street, and continue 1 block to the:

17. **Savoy,** built in 1889 by impresario Richard D'Oyly Carte
    as an adjunct to his theater.

    In August 1914, this hotel became something of a focal
    point for about 150,000 American tourists who found
    themselves stranded in Europe with the outbreak of World
    War I. Since many banks had closed, many of them were
    without money and unable to get a hotel room or steamer
    accommodations to return home. At the Savoy they formed
    a committee, later headed by Herbert Hoover, to contact
    American firms in London requesting a loan of money. Over
    the course of 6 weeks, $150,000,000 was raised, enabling
    some 120,000 Americans to return home. It's interesting to
    note that nearly everyone made good on his or her loan
    repayment—only about $300 was never repaid. One woman
    asked the committee for a written guarantee that the ship
    she'd be sailing on wouldn't be torpedoed by the Germans;
    it obliged by giving her exactly what she'd asked for! Hoover,
    a mining engineer, later headed a commission to provide
    relief in Belgium; his administrative abilities and record of
    public service eventually led him to the White House.

Continuing another block west along The Strand will bring you to the:

18. **Coal Hole,** 91 The Strand (☎ **0171/836-7503**), one of central London's largest pubs, established in the early 19th century for the coal haulers who unloaded boats on the Thames. Like many other pubs in and around the West End, the Coal Hole has numerous theatrical connections. In the mid-19th century, actor Edmund Kean would hire gangs of rowdies and get them drunk here before sending them to the Drury Lane's rival theaters to heckle the actors and cause trouble. Look for an inscription on one of the pub's interior wooden beams commemorating the Wolf Club, an informal group organized by Kean for men whose wives didn't allow them to sing in the bath.

Cross The Strand and continue straight ahead to Southampton Street. Walk up the hill to:

19. **Covent Garden Market,** a covered mall packed with interesting shops, sidewalk cafes, street performers, and tourists. Designed in the 1630s by Inigo Jones, one of London's most famous architects, this was a residential square that eventually fell into disrepair. All that remains is Jones's **St. Paul's Church** (not to be confused with St. Paul's Cathedral), on the west side of the square. The opening scene of George Bernard Shaw's *Pygmalion* (1913) takes place outside St. Paul's, where Professor Henry Higgins meets the flower seller Eliza Doolittle.

The Covent Garden Market (formerly the "convent garden" of Westminster Abbey stood here) housed a flower market from 1860 to 1974, when it was removed to Nine Elms. This is now a flourishing center for restaurants, cafes, bars, and, of course, pubs. The three pubs on the north side of the market (toward Covent Garden Underground Station) are all top picks for cozy comfort and lively atmosphere (as well as above-average pub grub). Any one of these would make a fine choice for ending your historic walk.

Cross to the opposite side of the market and walk up James Street to arrive at Covent Garden Underground Station.

Westminster & Whitehall

Start: Trafalgar Square.

Finish: Westminster Underground Station.

Time: 1½ hours, not including museum stops.

Best Time: When the museums are open, Monday to Saturday from 10am to 5:30pm and Sunday from 2 to 5:30pm.

Worst Time: Early Sunday, when the museums are closed.

W hitehall, the important thoroughfare that leads off Trafalgar Square, is the center of government. Much of the street was fronted by the old Palace of Whitehall until it burned down in 1698. Today, the home and foreign offices have a Whitehall address, as do a host of other government departments. The official residence of the prime minister is just steps away, on Downing Street, and the spectacular Houses of Parliament tower over Parliament Square, a short distance away.

This walk parallels the Thames and takes you past some of London's most famous buildings and monuments of historic and contemporary interest.

• • • • • • • • • • • • • • • •

Start at Trafalgar Square, which you can reach by taking the tube to the Charing Cross or Embankment Underground station (within 1 block of each other). Be careful of traffic as you cross to the center of:

1. **Trafalgar Square,** the heart of London. To the east is the City, London's financial center. To the north are Leicester Square and the commercial West End, London's entertainment and shopping areas. To the west is The Mall, the royal road that leads to Buckingham Palace. And to the south is Whitehall, the nation's street of government. At the center of pigeon-infested Trafalgar Square is:

2. **Nelson's Column,** one of the most famous monuments in London, commemorating Viscount Horatio Nelson's victory over a French and Spanish fleet at the Battle of Trafalgar (1805). The column is topped with a granite statue of Lord Nelson standing 17 feet high. It's so heavy that it had to be hoisted up in three sections.

   At the base of the column are the famous **Bronze Lions** and **Trafalgar Fountains.** The entire square is the site of London's large annual New Year's Eve party. Of the three other sculptures in Trafalgar Square, the most interesting is the:

3. **Equestrian statue of George IV,** which had been intended to top Marble Arch (now at the northeast corner of Hyde Park). George was known to his contemporaries as the First Gentleman of Europe, which led one poet to compose the following lampoon:

   > *A noble, nasty course he ran*
   > *Superbly filthy and fastidious,*
   > *He was the world's first gentleman*
   > *And made that appellation hideous.*

   Leave the square on the north side (again, be careful of fast-moving traffic) and walk to the:

4. **National Gallery** (☎ 0171/839-3321), a cupola-topped building that houses Britain's finest collection of paintings by world-class masters like Rembrandt, Raphael, Botticelli,

Westminster & Whitehall

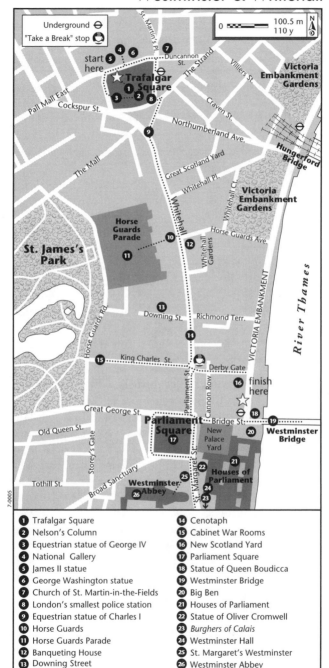

- ☉ Underground ⊖
- 🥐 "Take a Break" stop

0 ▭▭▭▭ 100.5 m
110 y

N

start here

Trafalgar Square

Pall Mall East

Cockspur St.

St. Martin's Pl.

Duncannon St.

The Strand

Villiers St.

Craven St.

Victoria Embankment Gardens

Northumberland Ave.

Great Scotland Yard

Whitehall Pl.

Hungerford Bridge

The Mall

Horse Guards Parade

Whitehall

Horse Guards Ave.

Whitehall Ct.

Victoria Embankment Gardens

St. James's Park

Horse Guards Rd.

Downing St.

Richmond Terr.

Whitehall Gardens

VICTORIA EMBANKMENT

River Thames

King Charles St.

Derby Gate

finish here

Parliament St.

Cannon Row

Great George St.

Old Queen St.

Storey's Gate

Bridge St.

Westminster Bridge

Parliament Square

New Palace Yard

Tothill St.

Broad Sanctuary

Westminster Abbey

St. Margaret St.

Houses of Parliament

7-0005

1	Trafalgar Square	**14**	Cenotaph
2	Nelson's Column	**15**	Cabinet War Rooms
3	Equestrian statue of George IV	**16**	New Scotland Yard
4	National Gallery	**17**	Parliament Square
5	James II statue	**18**	Statue of Queen Boudicca
6	George Washington statue	**19**	Westminster Bridge
7	Church of St. Martin-in-the-Fields	**20**	Big Ben
8	London's smallest police station	**21**	Houses of Parliament
9	Equestrian statue of Charles I	**22**	Statue of Oliver Cromwell
10	Horse Guards	**23**	*Burghers of Calais*
11	Horse Guards Parade	**24**	Westminster Hall
12	Banqueting House	**25**	St. Margaret's Westminster
13	Downing Street	**26**	Westminster Abbey

Goya, and Hogarth. The permanent collection, arranged by school, includes representative works from almost every major 13th- to 20th-century European artist. Temporary displays include selected works from the museum's own collection as well as some of the world's top traveling exhibits.

Works by such 19th-century French painters as Monet, Renoir, and Cézanne are especially popular. In the lower-floor galleries, you can see damaged paintings by great artists and even excellent forgeries.

Call ahead to take advantage of one of the regularly scheduled guided tours or guest lectures. The gallery offers special brochures, books, and educational events to focus attention on various aspects of its truly remarkable collection.

To the left of the main building is the **Sainsbury Wing,** opened in 1991. Several designs for the building were rejected after Prince Charles called them "a carbuncle on the face of Trafalgar Square." The one finally accepted was submitted by American architect Robert Venturi.

The gallery's main entrance is flanked by two small statues. On the left is the:

5. **James II statue,** created in 1686 by Grinling Gibbons, one of England's noted sculptors. The statue is widely regarded as one of the country's finest. James II ascended the throne in 1685 and quickly levied new, and unpopular, taxes. The king might have succeeded if he hadn't been so determined to restore Catholicism to England—a move that led to his deposition and forced exile in France, where he remained for the rest of his life. After James II died (1701), Benedictine monks kept his body embalmed in a French hearse for 92 years, waiting to see if the political and religious climate in England would change enough so that the former king could be buried in his native land. This never came to pass, however, and so James II was eventually buried at St-Germain.

On the right side of the gallery's entrance is the:

6. **George Washington statue,** a gift from the state of Virginia—a replica of the statue in the state capitol building in Richmond. The gift also included two boxes of earth

for the base of the statue, thereby ensuring that it would stand on American soil.

Walk clockwise around Trafalgar Square to the:

7. **Church of St. Martin-in-the-Fields** (☎ 0171/ 930-1862), on the northeastern corner. This popular London church (which may be the finest work of James Gibb) is famous for its spire-topped classical portico—a style often copied in 18th-century America. Begun in 1722, it's the burial site of several famous people, including furniture designer Thomas Chippendale and painters William Hogarth and Sir Joshua Reynolds. After visiting the church, go downstairs to the **London Brass Rubbing Centre,** where, for a small fee, you'll be provided with materials and instructions for making rubbings of replicas of medieval church brasses. The church is open to visitors Monday to Saturday from 10am to 6pm and Sunday from noon to 6pm.

On Monday and Tuesday at 1pm, the church usually holds free chamber-music concerts, often featuring works by well-known 19th-century composers. St. Martin's is also known for its exceptional choir; consider attending a full choral Sunday service.

Cross over to the square again and continue clockwise. At the southeast corner is a tiny cylindrical granite pillar, which is:

8. **London's smallest police station.** It was established in the 19th century as a secret observation post to enable the police to monitor marches and demonstrations held in the square. It barely accommodates one police officer plus a hand-cranked phone to summon help from nearby Scotland Yard, if necessary.

As you cross to enter Whitehall, you'll come to the:

9. **Equestrian statue of Charles I,** which dates from 1633 and was designed by French sculptor Hubert Le Sueur. Because Charles viewed himself as a just, divinely ordained monarch, he wanted the statue to convey this image. Thus, though the king was only 5 feet tall, he specified that the statue depict him as 6 feet in height.

Following Charles's 1649 execution, the statue was given to a scrap-metal dealer with instructions to destroy it. The dealer made a fortune selling souvenirs allegedly made from this statue, which he had, in fact, buried in his garden. When the monarchy was restored in 1660, the dealer was able to sell the undamaged statue to the new king, Charles II. It was placed here in 1765; the pedestal was designed by Sir Christopher Wren.

Proceed down Whitehall for 1 block; on your right will be two brightly suited guards on horseback. You've arrived at the:

10. **Horse Guards,** soldiers of the Queen's Household Division. Two regiments of the Household Cavalry Regiment alternate their guard here. If the soldiers are wearing scarlet tunics they belong to the Life Guards; if they're wearing blue tunics, they belong to the Blues and Royals. You can see the two regiments, which comprise the monarch's guard, daily here from 10am to 4pm. There's a small, usually un-crowded, changing-of-the-guard ceremony Monday to Saturday at 11am and Sunday at 10am. The most interesting event is probably the guard dismount, which takes place daily at 4pm.

Walk through the courtyard and under the Horse Guards Arch. Queen Victoria decreed that this arch should remain the official entrance to the royal palaces, even after the construction of Admiralty Arch. The parade ground on the other side of the arch is called:

11. **Horse Guards Parade**—the site of the Trooping the Colour, an impressive annual ceremony to celebrate the Queen's official birthday. The Queen is the colonel-in-chief of all seven regiments of the Household Division. The ceremony originated in the early days of land warfare, when military leaders used flags (colours) to rally their troops for battle. Since every soldier needed to be able to recognize his own unit's flag, it became the practice to carry ("troop") the colour down the ranks at the end of a day's march.

As you enter the Horse Guards Parade, look to your left. The building beyond the wall is the back of the prime minister's residence, **10 Downing St.** Your view from here is better than what is possible from the front (owing to security precautions).

Return to Whitehall and cross to the other side of the street. The building at the corner of Horse Guards Avenue is:

12. **Banqueting House,** the only remaining part of Whitehall Palace. Modeled by Inigo Jones on Sansovino's Library in Venice, it was completed in 1622. London's first purely Renaissance building, Banqueting House was intended for receptions, banquets, and theatrical performances. In 1635, Charles I commissioned Peter Paul Rubens to paint the ceilings, which glorified aspects of Charles's reign. These ceilings are breathtaking. Ironically, on January 30, 1649, that same king was brought here to be executed. Charles stepped out of an upstairs window onto a waiting scaffold and, in a steady voice, said, "I needed not have come here, and therefore I tell you (and I pray God it be not laid to your charge) that I am the martyr of the people." The king then placed his long hair under his cap, laid his neck on the chopping block, and stretched out his hands as a signal to the executioner to strike. His head was severed in a single blow, then held up to the crowds below, with the words "Behold the head of a traitor."

The light-brown brick building next to Banqueting House is the **Welsh Office.** The large building with the green roof, next door, is the **Ministry of Defence.**

Cross Whitehall again and walk 1 block to the iron gates on the right side. This is:

13. **Downing Street,** the address of the official residence of the British prime minister. Unlike most of the government buildings on Whitehall, which were erected in the 19th century, Downing Street is small in scale and lined with homes from 1680 to 1766. The street is named for Sir George Downing, a 17th-century member of Parliament and real-estate developer. Downing built this cul-de-sac of plain brick terrace houses around 1680; the only remaining houses are nos. 10, 11, and 12. No. 10, on the right side, has been home to prime ministers since 1732, when it was acquired by the Crown and offered as a personal gift to the First Lord of the Treasury, Sir Robert Walpole, who would accept it only as an office. No. 11 Downing St. is the

office and home of the Chancellor of the Exchequer. Extensive alterations were made to both buildings in the 1950s and 1960s. Although they look small, they actually contain sizable rooms and offices.

The obelisk marking the end of Whitehall and the beginning of Parliament Street is the:

14. **Cenotaph,** a tall white monument of Portland stone that now commemorates the dead of both World Wars. Often surrounded by flowers and wreaths, it was designed by Sir Edwin Lutyens and placed here in 1920. The word *cenotaph* derives from Greek words *kenos,* meaning "empty," and *taphos,* meaning "tomb." The monument's lines alternate between being slightly convex and concave, representing infinity. There are no religious symbols in the design; the only symbols are the flags of the three branches of the military and the standard of the merchant fleet.

Half a block ahead, turn right onto King Charles Street and walk 1 block to the:

15. **Cabinet War Rooms,** the government's underground World War II headquarters. Inside you can see the Cabinet Room, the Map Room, Prime Minister Winston Churchill's emergency bedroom, and the Telephone Room (where calls to Franklin D. Roosevelt were made). They've all been restored to their 1940s appearance—so accurately restored that there's even an open pack of cigarettes on the table. The rooms are open daily from 10am to 5:30pm. There is an admission charge.

Return to Parliament Street and cross over to the:

🍵 **Take a Break** **Red Lion Public House,** 48 Parliament St. (☎ **0171/930-5826**), frequented by members of Parliament and other civil servants. In fact, so many MPs come here that the pub rings a "divisional bell" to call the lawmakers back to Parliament before a vote is taken. The food is above average, and the usual beers are available.

Look up at the second-floor window for a medallion depicting Charles Dickens. At age 11, Dickens came to this pub to enjoy a pint of beer. The hero of *David Copperfield,* at the same age, came here and asked the proprietor, "What's your strongest ale?" He was told, "Aye, that'll be the genuine Stunning Ale."

Exit the Red Lion, turn left onto Derby Gate, and look down the road at the redbrick buildings of:

16. **New Scotland Yard,** the former home of England's top police force. When the foundation stone was laid in 1875, the intention was to build a lofty national opera house. A shortage of money stopped the project midway through until 1878, when the police proposed converting it into headquarters for their "A" division. In an ironic twist, the granite used for the new building was quarried by convicts from Dartmoor Prison. Described by architect Norman Shaw as "a very constabulary kind of castle," the finished structure provided 140 offices for the elite group. Since there were no elevators, senior officers were assigned rooms on the lower floors, while lower-ranking police officers had the higher floors. In 1967, Scotland Yard left this building in favor of new headquarters on Victoria Street.

Return to Parliament Street and walk 1 block ahead to:

17. **Parliament Square.** Laid out in the 1860s by Charles Barry, who also designed the new Houses of Parliament, the square was remodeled earlier in this century when its center was turned into a traffic island.

Turn left on Parliament Square and walk to the foot of Westminster Bridge. On your left, you'll see the:

18. **Statue of Queen Boudicca,** depicting the ancient British queen (died A.D. 60) and her daughters in a war chariot. The sculpture was created by Thomas Hornicroft in the 1850s and unveiled here in 1902. It's believed that Prince Albert lent his horses as models for this statue.

Now walk to the center of:

19. **Westminster Bridge,** a seven-arch cast-iron span that opened in 1750 and was rebuilt in 1862. The bridge's 84-foot width was considered exceptionally large at that time.

From the center of the bridge, look left, toward the City of London. It was this view that in 1802 inspired William Wordsworth to write:

> *Earth has not anything to show more fair:*
> *Dull would he be of soul who could pass by*
> *A sight so touching in its majesty:*
> *This City now doth like a garment wear*

> *The beauty of the morning; silent, bare,*
> *Ships, towers, domes, theatres, and temples lie*
> *Open unto the fields, and to the sky;*
> *All bright and glittering in the smokeless air.*
> —"Upon Westminster Bridge"

Admittedly, the view from the bridge has changed considerably since Wordsworth's day, though there are still some wonderful sights. For example, you can see the ornate back side of the Houses of Parliament. The balcony with the green canopy is the river terrace of the House of Commons; the one with the red canopy is the river terrace of the House of Lords.

Return toward Parliament Square and stand at the foot of:

20. **Big Ben,** the world's most famous clock tower. Contrary to popular belief, Big Ben refers neither to the tower nor to the clock; it's the name of the largest bell in the chime. Hung in 1856, the bell may have been named for either Sir Benjamin Hall (the commissioner of works when the bell was hung) or Ben Caunt (a popular prize fighter of the era who, at age 42, fought in a match that lasted 60 rounds). Each of the tower's four 200-foot-high clocks has a minute hand as large as a double-decker bus.

Walk clockwise around Parliament Square and stroll past the front of the:

21. **Houses of Parliament,** home of England's national legislature, which is made up of the **House of Commons** and **House of Lords.** Officially known as the Royal Palace of St. Stephen at Westminster, the Houses are located on the site of a royal palace built by Edward the Confessor before the Norman Conquest of 1066. During Edward's reign, this stretch of land along the Thames was surrounded by water and known as Thorny Island owing to the wild brambles that flourished there. The island had become sort of a pilgrimage site, celebrated for several miracles believed to have taken place there. When Edward ascended the throne, he chose this sacred spot to build the royal palace and church (Westminster Abbey). Later kings improved and enlarged the palace, which served as the official royal residence until 1512, when it was destroyed by fire.

The present Gothic-style building, with more than 1,000 rooms and 2 miles of corridors, was designed by Charles Barry and Augustus Pugin and completed in 1860. On May 10, 1941, the House of Commons was destroyed by German bombs but was rebuilt by Giles Gilbert Scott, the man who designed London's red telephone booths. Still, the House of Commons remains small. Only 346 of its 650 members can sit at any one time, while the rest crowd around the door and the Speaker's Chair. The ruling party and the opposition sit facing each other, two sword lengths apart. The House of Commons holds the political power in Parliament. The powers of the House of Lords were greatly curtailed in 1911. Unlike the Commons, whose members are elected, most of the members of the House of Lords are hereditary peers who inherit their seats. The Lords' opulently furnished chambers have an almost sacrosanct feel. Debates here aren't as interesting or lively as those in the more important House of Commons; however, a visit here will enable you to see the pageantry of Parliament.

You may watch debates from the **Strangers' Galleries** of Parliament's two houses. This can be rather interesting and is especially exciting during debates on particularly controversial topics.

The House of Commons is usually open to the public Monday to Thursday beginning at 4pm and Friday from 9:30am to 3pm. The House of Lords is generally open Monday to Thursday beginning about 3pm and on certain Fridays. For both houses, line up at St. Stephen's Entrance, just past the statue of Oliver Cromwell (see below). The debates often continue into the evening, but the lines become shorter after 6pm.

In the small garden in front of the Houses of Parliament is a:

22. **Statue of Oliver Cromwell,** a monument to England's only Lord Protector. Cromwell (1599–1658), who led the parliamentary armies during the Civil War that toppled Charles I, is depicted with a Bible in one hand and a sword in the other. When the statue was unveiled in 1899, it was vehemently criticized by Parliament's Irish representatives. Cromwell was hated in Ireland for his harsh policies, particularly the massacre of more than 30,000 men, women,

and children in Drogheda, followed by a trail of death and devastation from Wexford to Connaught. Motivated by religious as well as political considerations, he awarded vast tracts of land to his loyal followers, leaving less than one-ninth of Irish soil in Irish hands. Ultimately, Parliament refused to pay for the statue, and the prime minister at that time, Lord Rosebery, eventually paid for it himself. Do Cromwell's eyes appear to be downcast, as though ashamed of something? Look across the street, directly opposite the statue. Above the small doorway of the church is a small **bust of Charles I,** the monarch who was beheaded at Cromwell's instigation.

Continue ahead, keeping the Houses of Parliament to your left. Pass the Norman Tower (through which the Queen officially enters Parliament) and a little way along, turn left through the gates into Victoria Tower Gardens. Ahead you'll see the:

23. **Burghers of Calais** by August Rodin (1840–1917), commemorating the burghers' personal and perilous surrender of their city to Edward III in 1347. (Incidentally, Rodin was one of the greatest influences on British sculptors in the late 19th and early 20th centuries.)

Backtrack to the Cromwell statue. Behind the statue is:

24. **Westminster Hall,** the last remaining section of the old Houses of Parliament. A majestic vestige of Romanesque and Gothic architecture, the hall was built by William Rufus (ca. 1056–1100), the son of William the Conqueror. Something of a boaster, William Rufus once referred to this hall as nothing, as a mere bedchamber to his future projects . . . but there were to be no more.

Rebuilt from 1394 to 1402 for Richard II, the hall isn't much more than a large, rectangular banquet room, but it's noted for its magnificent oak hammerbeam roof. During the 15th and 16th centuries, some of England's best-known trials took place here—for example, those of Anne Boleyn and Sir Thomas More. Also tried here was Guy Fawkes, who conspired to blow up James I and the Houses of Parliament in the Gunpowder Plot of 1605. The 1649 trial of Charles I took place here as well, before an extremely reluctant panel of judges. Though he refused to accept the legality of this court, the king was found guilty; his sentence read: "for all which treasons and crimes this Court doth adjudge that sets as a tyrant, traitor, murderer, and publique enemy to the good people of this nation shall be put to death by the severing of his head from his body."

Oliver Cromwell was proclaimed Lord Protector here; more recently, this is where Sir Winston Churchill's body lay in state. Since the criminal courts moved to the Royal Courts of Justice in the late 19th century, Westminster Hall is now used only occasionally, primarily as a banquet hall for parliamentary functions. After a bomb killed an MP in 1979, entrance to Westminster Hall has become difficult. Tickets are available, on a limited basis, from your embassy.

With your back to the Cromwell statue, cross St. Margaret Street, turn left, and then turn right into the diminutive back door of:

25. **St. Margaret's Westminster,** a grand 16th-century church that's often mistaken for Westminster Abbey. Since 1614 St. Margaret's has been the parish church of the House of Commons but may be best known for its enormous East Window, a stained-glass masterpiece presented to Henry VII by Ferdinand and Isabella of Spain to commemorate the marriage of their daughter Catherine of Aragon to his eldest son, Arthur. On bright days, the East Window (above the altar) is brilliantly illuminated. The stained-glass gift was intended for Westminster Abbey, but by the time it arrived here from Spain, Arthur had died and his brother, Henry VIII, had already married Catherine.

Immediately inside the door, look to your right, where, almost hidden from view, is a commemorative **plaque** to Sir Walter Raleigh (1554–1618).

Exit St. Margaret's via the main door at the bottom of the church and walk a few steps to:

26. **Westminster Abbey** (☎ 0171/222-5152). The Benedictine abbey, which housed a community of monks as early as A.D. 750, was called Westminster (West Monastery) because of its location west of the City. In 1052, Edward the Confessor initiated construction of the present building, and it was consecrated in 1065. William the Conqueror was crowned at the abbey in 1066, and most British monarchs have continued to be crowned there. Many have been married and buried in the abbey as well. And, of course,

in September 1997 the abbey was the site of the funeral service for the adored Diana, Princess of Wales. When not in use, the Coronation Chair (built in 1300) sits behind the abbey's High Altar.

The **Poet's Corner** is the final resting place of some of Britain's most famous bards, including Geoffrey Chaucer, Robert Browning, and Alfred, Lord Tennyson.

The **Henry VII Chapel,** with its architectural extravagances and exquisite carvings, will take your breath away. Comprehensive "Super Tours" condense the abbey's 900-year history into 1½ hours; though these tours are expensive, many people believe that they're worth it.

The abbey is open Monday to Saturday from 9am to 5pm. The Royal Chapels are open Monday, Tuesday, Thursday, and Friday from 9am to 4:45pm; Wednesday from 9am to 8pm; and Saturday from 9am to 2pm and 3:30 to 5:45pm. Entrance to the abbey is free, but there's an admission charge to the Chapels (except Wednesday, the only time that photographs may be taken).

Exit Westminster Abbey, return to **Parliament Square,** and continue walking clockwise around the square. You've probably noticed that the square is surrounded by statues—the greatest concentration of outdoor sculptures in the city. Cross to the interior garden of Parliament Square. The statue nearest to you in the garden is of:

Sir Robert Peel, former prime minister and founder of London's Metropolitan Police Force, hence their nickname "Bobbies." The 1876 statue depicts Peel wearing a frock coat. In a House of Commons speech lasting over 4 hours, he introduced a bill for Catholic emancipation based on equality of civil rights. As he moved from point to point, cheers broke out so loud that they could be heard in Westminster Hall. Standing next to Peel, with his back toward you, is:

Benjamin Disraeli, England's first prime minister of Jewish ancestry. The statue was unveiled in 1883, on the second anniversary of Disraeli's death. He was said to have delighted in shocking others, a trait that led to hundreds of exaggerated stories about his behavior. One woman's claim that the prime minister appeared at a party wearing green velvet trousers and a black satin shirt became so popular that Disraeli himself wrote to a London newspaper editor to deny having ever owned a pair of green trousers in his life. Behind Disraeli, across the street, is:

Abraham Lincoln, the only non-British individual represented on the square. The monument, a gift from the city of Chicago, is an exact replica of the one in Lincoln Park.

In the northwest corner of Parliament Square, standing next to the statue of Disraeli, is the:

14th earl of Derby. Four pediment bronze reliefs depict highlights of the earl's career: at the House of Commons, as chancellor of the University of Oxford, at the Famine Relief Committee in Manchester, and as part of the Cabinet Council. Standing to Derby's right is:

Viscount Palmerston. Secretary of War for nearly 20 years, Palmerston is known for his nonpartisan politics. Tories thought him too Whiggish, and Whigs suspected him of Toryism. He was sympathetic to the Greek struggle for independence and consistently advocated and voted for Catholic emancipation, which he predicted "would give peace to Ireland."

Continue walking to the north side of Parliament Square, where you'll see:

Gen. Jan Smuts, who appears to be ice-skating. An expert in early guerrilla warfare, Smuts commanded the Boer forces in the Second South African War (the Boer War). He later commanded the South African forces in World War I and held many South African government posts, including that of prime minister.

Returning to the northeast corner of Parliament Square, you'll see:

Sir Winston Churchill, one of Britain's greatest statesmen, created by Ivor Roberts-Jones in 1973. Leaning on a stick, bulldog fashion, the World War II prime minister is looking across the street toward the Houses of Parliament.

Cross Parliament Square to the corner of Parliament Street, cross over the pedestrian crossing, and keep walking ahead onto Budget Street. Two blocks along on the left is Westminster Underground Station.

St. James's

Start: Green Park Underground Station.
Finish: Green Park Underground Station.
Time: 2 hours.
Best Time: Monday to Saturday from 9:30am to 5pm.
Worst Time: Sundays, when shops are closed.

This small corner of London, nestled between Green Park and St. James's Park, has long been a favorite of the upper classes. The area called St. James's emerged around the Royal Palace of Henry VIII. Believing that it would be advantageous to be close to power, the wealthy erected splendid homes for themselves near the palace. St. James's heyday was in the 18th and 19th centuries, when most of the houses, shops, and clubs were built, many with riches acquired throughout the empire.

The British class system is an outgrowth of the nation's past, though it may not be obvious to a visitor. The Royal Family remains a potent symbol of the importance the British attach to birth. More than three-quarters of the members of the House of Lords are hereditary peers, meaning that they inherit their seats as a birthright. Even today, many of England's nobility are wealthy simply because they own land that has been passed down for generations—land that was given to their ancestors by a king or queen hundreds of years ago. Many of the buildings on this tour that may be unremarkable for their architecture are spectacular for the culture that they represent.

● ● ● ● ● ● ● ● ● ● ● ● ● ● ● ●

Leave Green Park Underground Station via the Buckingham Palace/Ritz Hotel exit. Turn right on Piccadilly and walk toward the Ritz. Just after the telephone boxes, turn right and go through the iron gates onto an unmarked pedestrian walkway called Queen's Walk. On your right is:

1. **Green Park,** owned by the Crown estate and so named because it contains no flower beds. Although the reason for this lack isn't precisely known, one popular story has it that Charles II was walking here one day with his entourage when he announced that he planned to pick a flower to give to the most beautiful lady present. When he gave it to a milkmaid from the local dairy, Queen Catherine became so enraged that she ordered all the park's flowers removed. Over the years, Green Park has been the setting for duels, balloon ascents, and other events; to celebrate the peace of Aix-la-Chapelle in 1749, a spectacular fireworks display was arranged, and for this occasion Handel composed his "Music for the Royal Fireworks." Green Park is popular with picnickers, strollers, and patient British sun worshipers.

   Continue down Queen's Walk and notice the still-functioning gas lamps lining the path. After the fifth lamp, turn left down the passage that goes under several residential buildings (which, incidentally, are some of London's most expensive apartments). After emerging on the other side, turn right. Just opposite you'll see the:

2. **Stafford Hotel,** 16–18 St. James's Place, favored by James Thurber since his first stay in 1955. Thurber was admired in England and relished the attention he received. He believed that there was something about the country that enabled its writers to achieve a ripe old age. By contrast, he remarked that most male writers in America had died before they reached the age of 60; those who lived beyond no longer had anything to say but often said it anyway.

   Continue 1 block to the grand house at the end of the street, which is:

3. **Spencer House,** 27 St. James's Place (☎ **0171/409-0526**), the ancestral home of the late Diana, Princess of Wales. The house, built for Earl John Spencer, was begun in 1765 by John Vardy, a pupil of William Kent, but was completed by James Stuart after the shell had been constructed. The working gas lamps and torch extinguishers around the front door are typical of this earlier age. The house hasn't been used as a private residence since 1927, though it remained the property of the trustees of the 8th Earl Spencer's marriage settlement. In the 1980s, Jacob Rothschild took over the lease and had the building restored as a favor to Diana. Now operated by the Spencer Trust, it's used primarily for private functions. Since the worst time to take this tour is a Sunday, it's unfortunate that the house is open to the public only on that day from 10:45am to 4:45pm. A guided tour is scheduled every 15 minutes, and there's an admission charge.

The building next door to the left is:

4. **28 St. James's Place,** the former home of William Huskisson. A treasurer of the British navy in the early 19th century and arch-rival of the duke of Wellington, Huskisson may best be remembered as the first person to be fatally injured by a steam-powered train; the accident occurred at the opening ceremony for the Liverpool–Manchester railway in 1830. It seems that Huskisson tended to be accident-prone.

Continue farther along St. James's Place where, on your left, is:

5. **11 St. James's Place,** the former home of Robert Cruikshank, one of London's most beloved satirical cartoonists. In the early 19th century, Cruikshank and his brother George created the cartoon characters Tom and Jerry—two stylish and bawdy young men who were featured in a series of engravings called "Life in London" in 1820 to 1821. The cartoons, which were popular in both England and America, were the model for today's popular and always-at-war animated cat and mouse.

Next door you'll see:

6. **10 St. James's Place,** where writer Oscar Wilde kept an apartment in the 1890s. It was here that Wilde met with

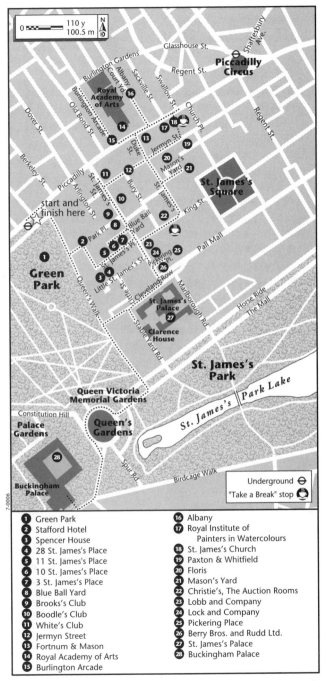

1. Green Park
2. Stafford Hotel
3. Spencer House
4. 28 St. James's Place
5. 11 St. James's Place
6. 10 St. James's Place
7. 3 St. James's Place
8. Blue Ball Yard
9. Brooks's Club
10. Boodle's Club
11. White's Club
12. Jermyn Street
13. Fortnum & Mason
14. Royal Academy of Arts
15. Burlington Arcade
16. Albany
17. Royal Institute of Painters in Watercolours
18. St. James's Church
19. Paxton & Whitfield
20. Floris
21. Mason's Yard
22. Christie's, The Auction Rooms
23. Lobb and Company
24. Lock and Company
25. Pickering Place
26. Berry Bros. and Rudd Ltd.
27. St. James's Palace
28. Buckingham Palace

several young men who testified against him at his "gross indecency" trial in 1895. (For more information on Wilde, see Stop 16 in Walking Tour 10.)

A few doors farther down the street is:

7. **3 St. James's Place,** occupied by composer Frédéric Chopin (1810–49) for 1 month in 1848. He was living here at the time he gave his last public performance—at Guildhall.

At the end of St. James's Place, turn left onto St. James's Street, walk a few yards, and turn left again into:

8. **Blue Ball Yard,** a delightful cobblestone courtyard from 1741. Named for the Blue Ball Inn that once stood here, the yard is now the setting for some of London's most picturesque residences. You can see that these two-story buildings were once used as stables; look for the silhouetted images of horses' heads that hang above names such as Farlap and Copenhagen.

Return to St. James's Street, turn left, and cross Park Place. The next couple of blocks along St. James's Street are some of the swankiest in the world. Here are located some of London's most exclusive gentlemen's clubs. For centuries, these bastions of privilege have provided lodging, food, drink, and good company for the well-to-do. Women aren't permitted on the premises of most of these clubs, and aspiring members may have to wait many years to be accepted. None of these clubs displays its name; they want to discourage attention from the general public, including sightseers (who aren't permitted inside).

The ornate building on the far left corner of St. James's Street and Park Place is:

9. **Brooks's Club,** 60 St. James's St. This 1778 building was constructed for the Whig politicians who supported the American revolutionaries. The Whigs, who viewed the revolutionaries as fellow Englishmen, also wanted to escape the rule of George III. One of the club's objectives was to collect money for "the widows, orphans, and aged parents of our beloved American fellow-subjects, who, faithful to the character of Englishmen, preferring death to slavery, were for that reason only inhumanly murdered by the king's troops at or near Lexington and Concord."

With your back toward Brooks's, look across the street at the white building. This is:

10. **Boodle's Club,** 28 St. James's St. This 1775 building is named after one of its earliest managers, Edward Boodle, a man who squandered his large inheritance and delighted in teaching young men to drink heavily. It's not surprising that the club early on acquired a reputation for heavy gambling and good food. Past members have included historian Edward Gibbon, author of *The Decline and Fall of the Roman Empire;* abolitionist William Wilberforce; socialite George Bryan ("Beau") Brummell; and the duke of Wellington. The room on the third floor, to the left of the venetian window, is the "undress dining room" for dining in informal clothes. Behind the venetian window is the club's main salon, which is 1½ stories high.

Continue 1 block along St. James's and cross at the pedestrian crossing. Continue along the right side of the street to the white stone building just past National Westminster Bank. This is:

11. **White's Club,** 37–38 St. James's St., the oldest and grandest of the St. James's gentlemen's clubs. This one was established on the site of White's Chocolate House, in a building that dates to 1788. The club acquired an early reputation for around-the-clock gambling; as one popular gentlemen's magazine noted: "There is nothing, however trivial or ridiculous, which is not capable of producing a bet."

One 1750 report tells of a man who happened to collapse near the door of this club. He was carried upstairs and immediately became the object of bets as to whether or not he was dead! One rainy day, it's said that Lord Arlington bet £3,000 on which of two drops of rain would reach the bottom of a window pane first. Bets were placed on births, deaths, marriages, public events, and politics—almost anything that came up in conversation or caused an argument.

The club has a long conservative history and still claims many political Tories as members. Prince Charles is affiliated with this club. When the Labour political leader Aneurin Bevan, who had once described all Tories as "lower than vermin," dined here in 1950, he was kicked in the bottom by a member (who was then forced to resign).

Walk two doors back on St. James's Street and turn left onto:

12. **Jermyn Street,** one of the world's most expensive shopping streets. The small stores lining it are famous for their long-standing service to upper-class and royal clients. Most display Royal Warrants above their front doors—coats of arms that are given to those who provide goods to members of the Royal Family. On your right, the colorful shop front of the royal shirtmakers, **Turnbull & Asser,** 71–72 Jermyn St., is especially noteworthy, as is **Taylor of Old Bond Street,** 74 Jermyn St., a 19th-century-era beauty salon specializing in herbal remedies and aromatherapy.

Halfway down Jermyn Street, turn left onto Duke Street St. James's. The lime-colored building on your right is:

13. **Fortnum & Mason,** 181 Piccadilly (☎ 0171/734-8040), the royal grocers. Enter the store at the Duke Street entrance to be greeted by one of the formally attired attendants.

Fortnum's, as it's affectionately called, was started by William Fortnum, a footman in Queen Anne's household. Since part of his job entailed replenishing the royal candelabras, Fortnum supplemented his income by selling the queen's partially used candles. When he retired in 1707, Fortnum opened this upscale grocery store with his friend Hugh Mason. It was an immediate success, and by 1788 the shop had become world famous, shipping preserved foods and traditional specialties to English military, diplomatic, and other personnel overseas. Visitors to London's Great Exhibition of 1851—the first world's fair—came to Fortnum's to marvel at the exotic fruits and prepared foods and to buy picnic hampers—a tradition that survives to this day.

On June 16, 1886, a smartly dressed American man came to Fortnum's to meet with the head of grocery purchasing. Introducing himself as "a food merchant from Pittsburgh," the American gave Fortnum's grocer his first taste of horseradish, chili sauce, and tomato ketchup. Excited by these new tastes, the grocer enthusiastically said, "I think, Mr. Heinz, we will take them all." H. J. Heinz had arrived.

Exit Fortnum's main doors onto Piccadilly and look up at the glockenspiel clock above the front entrance. If you're lucky enough to be here on the hour, you'll hear the clock chime the "Eton Boat Song," as the doors swing open to reveal little figures depicting Mr. Fortnum and Mr. Mason.

With your back to Fortnum & Mason, cross Piccadilly. The large building to your right is the:

14. **Royal Academy of Arts,** Burlington House, Piccadilly (☎ **0171/439-4996**). Founded in 1768, the Royal Academy is the oldest society in England dedicated exclusively to the fine arts. Displayed are works by Reynolds, Turner, Gainsborough, Constable, and Stubbs. Michelangelo's *Madonna and Child with the Infant St. John* is also here; it's one of only four of the master's sculptures outside Italy. The Academy, which moved to this site in 1868, is also well known for its annual summer exhibition, where contemporary works are shown and (often) sold. It's open Monday to Saturday from 10am to 6pm, and there's an admission charge.

Burlington House is the last of half a dozen upper-class mansions that lined Piccadilly in the mid-17th century. Piccadilly is now one of the city's major commercial thoroughfares; its name derives from the ornate "piccadill" collars worn by fashionable men in the 17th century. One of the best-known piccadill makers lived in this area.

To the left of the Royal Academy is the:

15. **Burlington Arcade,** one of the world's oldest shopping malls; it was designed by Samuel Ware and built in 1819 by Lord George Cavendish "for the gratification of the public and to give employment to Industrious females." Lord Cavendish lived next door in Burlington House and reputedly built the arcade to stop bawdy Londoners from throwing oyster shells into his garden.

Tailcoated watchmen, called beadles, continue to enforce the arcade's original code of behavior, making sure that visitors don't run, shout, sing, hum, or whistle.

Backtrack to Piccadilly and turn left. Walk past Burlington House and take the first left turn into the courtyard of the:

16. **Albany,** a 1770 Georgian apartment building that's one of London's most prestigious addresses. Built for the 1st Viscount Melbourne, the Albany was sold in 1802 to a

young developer named Alexander Copland, who commissioned architect Henry Holland to convert the building into flats for single young men—actually, bachelor apartments. Many authors, playwrights, and poets have lived here, including Graham Greene, Aldous Huxley, J. B. Priestly, and Lord Byron. (Even Oscar Wilde's fictitious Jack Worthing—who was Jack in the country but Ernest in town—lived at the Albany, as his calling card stated in *The Importance of Being Earnest*.) Pursuing her 9-month infatuation with Lord Byron, Lady Caroline Lamb once managed to enter his Albany apartment disguised as a pageboy. Lady Caroline didn't find Byron at home, but she wrote "Remember me" on the flyleaf of one of his books. Byron was so upset by this invasion of his privacy that he penned a poem ending with these words:

> *Remember thee! Aye doubt it not,*
> *Thy husband too shall think of thee,*
> *By neither shall thou be forgot,*
> *Thou false to him, thou fiend to me!*

Continue a half block down Piccadilly and look across the street at the:

17. **Royal Institute of Painters in Watercolours,** 195 Piccadilly (above United Airlines), the former headquarters of the British School of Water Colour Painting. The school was opened in 1831, and this building was constructed specifically for its use in 1882. Between every window you can see busts of those who founded the school, including that of J. M. W. Turner. When the school's lease on this building expired in 1970, it moved to Pall Mall.

Cross Piccadilly at the traffic light and enter the courtyard of:

18. **St. James's Church,** 197 Piccadilly (☎ **0171/734-4511**), a postwar reconstruction of one of Sir Christopher Wren's loveliest churches. Consecrated in 1684 and known as the Visitors Church, St. James's is indeed one of the city's most tourist-friendly chapels.

To the right of the entrance is an old **American Indian catalpa tree** and a plaque reading: "When tired or sad an Amerindian will hug a tree to get in touch with earth's energy—why not you?" Across from the tree, on the church wall, is a pulpit formerly used for outdoor noontime sermons. Today, the noise from cars on Piccadilly would probably make this impractical.

Enter St. James's Church and turn left into the main chapel. The interior of this church is exceptionally elegant; Corinthian columns support splendid barrel vaults decorated with ornate plasterwork. In 1684, diarist John Evelyn expressed his view that "there was no altar anywhere in England, nor has there been any abroad more handsomely adorned."

The marble **font** at the rear left corner of the chapel is the church's greatest prize. Created by Grinling Gibbons, London's most famous Stuart-era sculptor, the intricate stem represents Adam and Eve standing on either side of the tree of life. Poet William Blake, among others, was baptized here.

The large **organ** at the back of the church was made in 1685 for James II's Chapel Royal in nearby Whitehall and given to St. James's in 1691. Its case was carved by Grinling Gibbons. Two British composers, John Blow and Henry Purcell, reportedly tried the organ soon after its installation. When it was being repaired in 1852, a miniature coffin containing a bird was discovered inside the instrument.

Near the fourth window on the left side of the church is a **plaque** honoring Sir Richard Croft, a 19th-century royal physician. His story is rather tragic. In 1817, Croft was caring for the pregnant Princess Charlotte—the only child of the Prince Regent. Because of pregnancy-related complications, Croft decided to bleed the princess and permit her very little food, hoping that this would cure her of a "morbid excess of animal spirits." After being in labor for 50 hours, Charlotte gave birth to a stillborn baby, and the princess died a few hours later. Although the Prince Regent published a kindly tribute to Croft, the physician's reputation was ruined. In February 1818, Croft was asked to care for another pregnant woman whose symptoms resembled those of Princess Charlotte. Before the birth, however, the doctor found a pistol hanging on the wall of the woman's house and shot himself.

Leave the church via the Jermyn Street exit, located directly opposite the door you entered. There you'll find the:

Take a Break **Wren at St. James's,** 35 Jermyn St. (☎ 0171/437-9419), is a delightful and inexpensive health-food cafe and art gallery where you can enjoy carrot soup, fresh salads, a variety of sandwiches, and vegetarian lasagna.

After you leave the Wren, turn right on Jermyn Street. Just ahead is:

19. **Paxton & Whitfield,** 93 Jermyn St. (☎ 0171/930-0259), a store known not only for its cheeses but also for its terrific meat and fruit pies.

A few doors down is:

20. **Floris,** 89 Jermyn St. (☎ 0171/930-2885), the city's most exclusive perfumery. Notice the almost garishly large Royal Warrant above the door. Floris has been making its wealthy clients smell nice since 1810; this old shop is something of a scent museum, and you may enjoy going in to see the delightful old display cases.

Continue on Jermyn Street for half a block and turn left onto Duke Street St. James's. Walk 1 block and turn left into:

21. **Mason's Yard,** a small square with some interesting associations. The surveyor's office on your left, at 6 Mason's Yard, was once the site of the Indica Art Gallery, a center for the 1960s avant-garde movement. Shareholders in the gallery included Beatles Paul McCartney and John Lennon. It was here that John Lennon and Yoko Ono first met.

Diagonally across the courtyard, to your left, is the **Directors Lodge Club,** 13 Mason's Yard (☎ 0171/930-2540). Now a hostess bar for men, this was formerly the site of a bar called the Scotch of St. James, a 1960s favorite haunt of the Beatles, Rolling Stones, and others. It's claimed that Jimi Hendrix was "discovered" here.

Continue along Duke Street St. James's, past upscale art galleries; after 1 block turn right onto King Street. Half a block ahead on your right is:

22. **Christie's, The Auction Rooms,** 8 King St. (☎ 0171/839-9060), one of the world's best-known fine-art auctioneers. Established in 1766 by James Christie, a former navy

midshipman, the establishment was moved to this location by the founder's son, James Jr., in 1823.

Opposite the auction house is the:

☕ **Take a Break** **Golden Lion Pub,** 25 King St. (☎ **0171/930-7227**). A recent costly refurbishing has transformed this into one of the nicest pubs in the neighborhood. Fortunately, the quality of the food hasn't changed. Good pub lunches are served with Tetley, Burton, and other English ales; each month there's a "guest" beer.

Walk 1 block and turn left onto St. James's Street. Half a block down on your left is:

23. **Lobb and Company,** 9 St. James's St. (☎ **0171/930-5849**), shoe and bootmakers to the royals and the gentry. From left to right, the Royal Warrants above the door are from Queen Elizabeth, the duke of Edinburgh, and the Prince of Wales. Inside, you can usually see a variety of wooden moldings of clients' feet used for custom-made shoes. Hidden in the shop's vaults are centuries-old as well as contemporary moldings of famous royal feet, including those of Prince Charles, the late Princess Diana, Queen Elizabeth, and Prince Philip.

A few doors down is:

24. **Lock and Company,** 6 St. James's St. (☎ **0171/930-5849**). Located at these premises since 1764, this hatmaker has covered some of the world's most important heads. Lord Nelson ordered a hat from Lock with a built-in eye patch; the duke of Wellington bought from Lock the famous plumed hat that he wore at the Battle of Waterloo. It's said that the top hat was designed here in 1797. Its height caused such a furor that the first wearer was arrested and fined £50 for "going about in a manner calculated to frighten timid people." In 1850, William Coke, a gamekeeper, ordered from Lock a hard domed hat for protection while chasing poachers. Produced by Thomas and William Bowler, Lock's chief suppliers, the hat became known worldwide as a bowler. But around St. James's, the hat was called a coke, after the man who had ordered it.

The narrow alleyway three doors down on your left is:

25. **Pickering Place,** the address of the Texas Legation from
    1842 to 1845. Before Texas became a U.S. state, the Re-
    public of Texas had its own diplomatic mission in Britain,
    and a lone star on the wall of the alley commemorates this
    fact.

    Enter the alley and walk to the delightfully quiet **en-
    closed courtyard.** The buildings surrounding you were con-
    structed in the 1730s by William Pickering. Although you
    can't see them, you're standing over a series of cellars where
    Louis-Napoléon Bonaparte, later to become Napoléon III,
    may have plotted his return to France during his exile in
    the 1840s.

    Return to St. James's Street; the building immediately
    to your left is:

26. **Berry Bros. and Rudd Ltd.,** 3 St. James's St. (☎ 0171/
    396-9600), wine and spirit merchants with Royal Warrants.
    If you drink Cutty Sark whiskey, you may recall the Berry
    Bros. name on every bottle. Notice the 18th-century wooden
    shop front, which was heavily scratched by stones churned
    up by the wheels of passing carriages. Founded in 1696,
    Berry Bros. began as a grocery store; inside is a huge set of
    scales that was brought in for weighing coffee. Uncommon
    in their time, the scales became popular with customers
    who often weighed themselves on them. For about 300 years,
    nearly 30,000 local people have weighed themselves here;
    their weights have been recorded in large ledgers. In addi-
    tion to Lord Byron, Lord Nelson, and Lady Hamilton,
    we now have the recorded weight of William IV (189 lbs.,
    in boots); Queen Victoria's father, the duke of Kent (232
    lbs.); and others. The 4th Baron Rivers weighed himself
    and had it written down almost 500 times. An entry for
    July 27, 1864, reads: "12 stone 4 lbs. at 1.30; 12 stone
    5 lbs. at 2pm after two chops and a pint of sherry." [*Note:*
    1 stone = 14 lbs.]

    Walk half a block to the end of St. James's Street, which
    terminates at:

27. **St. James's Palace,** the official residence of the mon-
    arch. The palace, which dates from the reign of Henry VIII,
    was the main residence of England's kings and queens for
    more than 300 years until Queen Victoria moved the royal

residence to Buckingham Palace in 1837. At the time of this writing, the palace is home to Prince Charles and the two princes, William and Harry. It was in the chapel here that in September 1997 the body of Princess Diana lay, awaiting her funeral, while thousands of people stood in line for hours and hours to sign books of condolence.

Named for a convent that once stood on this site, St. James's Palace is today the headquarters of the Yeomen of the Guard and contains the Lord Chamberlain's office. Until recently, the ceremoniously garbed sentries who guard the front gate used to carry only swords. However, threats from the Irish Republican Army and others prompted the switch to bayonetted machine guns. By tradition, the stone-faced sentries aren't supposed to talk. Feel free to take their pictures and try to make them laugh.

Turn right at the palace, walk to Cleveland Row, and turn left onto Stable Yard Road. Pause at the security barrier to look at **Clarence House,** the home of Her Majesty Queen Elizabeth, the Queen Mother. Backtrack on Stable Yard Road to Cleveland Row and turn left. Take the small Milk Maid's Passage to Queen's Walk. Turn left and walk down to The Mall ("Mell") and then right to:

28. Buckingham Palace, the home of Elizabeth II and Prince Philip. Originally owned by the duke of Buckingham, the house was converted into a royal residence by George IV. John Nash, one of London's most productive architects, directed the renovation. The work was still not finished when Queen Victoria moved there in 1837, and successive modifications have enlarged it to almost 600 rooms. The popularity of the palace itself isn't due to its age or its architecture—it's neither old nor spectacular. But as home of one of the world's few remaining celebrated monarchs, the building is of symbolic interest. Although the public view is of the rather plain neo-Georgian east front (added by Sir Aston Webb in 1913), the best view may be from the back, where the Queen's famous garden parties are held.

The Changing of the Guard ceremony, performed by five rotating regiments of the Queen's Foot Guards, is held here daily at 11:30am in summer and on alternate days from August to March. (The ceremony isn't held during bad weather or at the time of major state events.)

The ceremony actually begins at 11am when the St. James's Palace detachment of the Old Guard assembles in Friary Court at St. James's Palace. The captain of the Queen's Guard performs an inspection, then the drummers beat the call "The point of war," and the colour is brought on. This done, the corps of drummers lead the way and the St. James's detachment march off via The Mall to Buckingham Palace.

Meanwhile, the Buckingham Palace detachment of the Old Guard has fallen in and been inspected. It's joined by the St. James's Old Guard, which assembles to the right in the forecourt of Buckingham Palace.

At 11:30am the New Guard approaches the palace from the Birdcage Walk, enters the grounds via the north center gate, marches to a central position, and executes a left-form, halting in front of the Old Guard.

As the two groups stand facing each other, the captains of the Guard march toward each other and perform the ceremony of handing over the palace keys. Symbolically, the responsibility for the security of the palace has now passed from the Old to the New Guard. At 12:05pm, the Old Guard exits the palace grounds via the center gate and marches back to the barracks.

Since 1993, guided tours of the public rooms at Buckingham Palace have been available during August and September (when the Royal Family is away for their holidays). There's an admission charge.

Return to Queen's Walk and follow it for the whole length, then turn left onto Piccadilly. Half a block along on the left is Green Park Underground Station.

The East End

Start: Aldgate Underground Station.

Finish: Aldgate East Underground Station.

Time: 2 hours, moderately paced.

Best Time: Sunday to Friday until 1pm.

Worst Time: Saturdays and evenings after 5pm.

T he East End, an amorphous area hugging the City of London's eastern edge, encompasses two adjacent territories: Whitechapel and Spitalfields. From its beginning, the East End has been one of London's poorest areas. Traditionally, it was undesirable because the prevailing winds and the west-to-east flow of the Thames carried diseases from the City and the hamlets to the west. Living on the "wrong" side of the City was dangerous indeed.

Spitalfields was once England's silk-weaving center, established in the 16th and 17th centuries by French and Flemish weavers. By the end of the 18th century, about 17,000 looms were in operation, making weaving one of the largest businesses in the East End. Today little, if any, weaving is still done, but there are many reminders of the area's earlier history.

Many of the East End's residents have been newly arrived immigrants from Ireland and the Continent, and in more recent years, from the Indian subcontinent and the Caribbean. At the turn of the century the area was home to most of England's Jewish population, almost 90% by 1914, who lived in Spitalfields, Whitechapel, and St. George's to the east. They brought to the area a lively intellectual life. However, few Jews still live there today.

The East End's most notorious connection is, of course, with Jack the Ripper, whose infamous series of still-unsolved murders took place in Whitechapel in 1888.

• • • • • • • • • • • • • • • • • •

Exit Aldgate Underground Station and turn right to arrive at the:

1. **Church of St. Botolph Aldgate.** Although a church has stood on this site for a thousand years, this building (designed by George Dance the elder) dates from 1740. The attractive ceiling is adorned with figures created by J. F. Bentley (1839–1902), the English architect who designed the Roman Catholic Westminster Cathedral. On the wall of the right aisle is a charming 18th-century wood carving of King David playing his harp. Note the realistic miniature musical instruments on either side of him.

   Exit the church and turn right onto Aldgate High Street. Cross over the two street crossings, bearing right into Duke's Place. Just ahead on your left is:

2. **Sir John Cass's Foundation School.** The school was founded in 1669 to educate both boys and girls. In 1710, Alderman Sir John Cass (1661–1718) agreed to make a financial grant to support the school, but while drawing up a second will to provide additional support he suffered a fatal hemorrhage. His blood stained the quill pen with which he was writing. This tragedy is still commemorated each year on Founder's Day (early February), when the pupils are given quill pens, stained red, that they wear on their coat lapel buttonholes.

   Continue walking along Duke's Place; after another block it becomes Bevis Marks. Half a block farther on the left is the entrance to the:

3. **Bevis Marks Synagogue** (☎ 0171/626-1274). Founded in 1701, this is England's oldest synagogue. It has

The East End

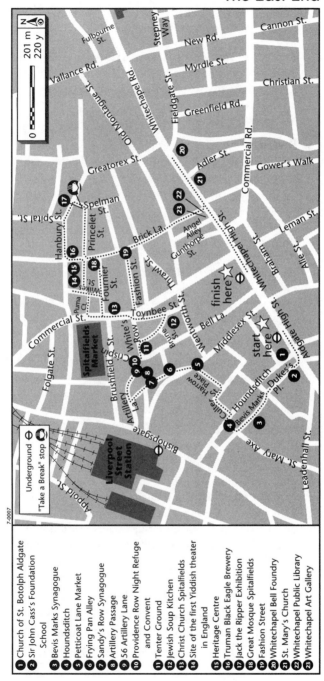

1. Church of St. Botolph Aldgate
2. Sir John Cass's Foundation School
3. Bevis Marks Synagogue
4. Houndsditch
5. Petticoat Lane Market
6. Frying Pan Alley
7. Sandy's Row Synagogue
8. Artillery Passage
9. 56 Artillery Lane
10. Providence Row Night Refuge and Convent
11. Tenter Ground
12. Jewish Soup Kitchen
13. Christ Church Spitalfields
14. Site of the first Yiddish theater in England
15. Heritage Centre
16. Truman Black Eagle Brewery
17. Jack the Ripper Exhibition
18. Great Mosque Spitalfields
19. Fashion Street
20. Whitechapel Bell Foundry
21. St. Mary's Church
22. Whitechapel Public Library
23. Whitechapel Art Gallery

7-0007

81

been in continuous use and its interior has changed very little over the years. It's open Sunday to Wednesday from 11:30am to 1pm and Friday from 11:30am to 12:30pm; a guided tour begins on each of those days at 11:30am.

Backtrack to Bevis Marks and turn left. Continue 2 blocks, cross the pedestrian walkway, and head left into St. Mary Axe. The street at the end is:

4. **Houndsditch.** This street runs along the site of the moat that once bounded the City wall. The origin of the street's name isn't known, but one "colorful" suggestion was made by 17th-century historian John Stow. He conjectured that the street was named "from that in old time, when the same lay open, much filth (conveyed forth of the City) especially dead dogges were laid there or cast."

Cross over at the traffic lights and turn right along Houndsditch. Take the first left into Cutler Street and follow it around to the right. Half a block ahead, turn left into Harrow Place and continue until you get to Middlesex Street, which is the site of the:

5. **Petticoat Lane Market.** A lively street market takes place here every Sunday beginning at 8am (the best time to see it). This street was known as Peticote Lane as early as 1608, probably because of those who sold old clothes here. By the 1830s, when the name had been changed to Middlesex Street, it had become one of London's largest street markets.

Turn left into Middlesex Street and, staying on the right side of the street, walk 4 blocks to arrive at:

6. **Frying Pan Alley.** The frying pan was the emblem used by braziers and ironmongers during the Middle Ages; undoubtedly, the presence of such tradesmen in this area accounts for the alley's name. There's little of interest here today.

Continue ahead on Middlesex Street to Sandy's Row. One block ahead on the right will bring you to:

7. **Sandy's Row Synagogue,** 4A Sandy's Row (☎ 0171/ 253-8311). This building was originally a Huguenot church but in 1867 was leased to Dutch Jews who used it for their Society of Kindness and Truth. You can view it by appointment.

Continue ahead on Sandy's Row and turn right into Artillery Lane. Half a block later, turn right into Parliament Court and then left into:

8. **Artillery Passage.** In the 16th century this whole area comprised open fields outside the City walls and was used primarily for recreational purposes. In 1537, Henry VIII granted a Royal Warrant to the Honourable Artillery Company and later permitted them to practice in these fields. Several streets in this area bear the name Artillery—derived from the Artillery barracks that once stood here.

Continue walking along Artillery Passage until you reach Artillery Lane. Two doors along on the right will bring you to:

9. **56 Artillery Lane.** This building dates from 1756 and is widely considered to be the finest Georgian storefront in London.

Opposite you'll see a large building on the left; this is the:

10. **Providence Row Night Refuge and Convent,** built in 1868 and run by the order of the Sisters of Mercy. During the late 19th century, the order provided lodging "to the destitute from all parts, without distinction of creed, colour, and country."

Cross Crispin Street and enter White's Row; take the first right turn into:

11. **Tenter Ground.** Until the 1820s, this was a wide-open space used for drying fabric; the cloth was attached to large hooks and then stretched over wooden frames. From this practice came the expression "to be on tenter hooks."

At the end of Tenter Ground, turn left into Brune Street. Walk 1 block to the:

12. **Jewish Soup Kitchen.** Opened in 1902 (the year 5662 in the Jewish calendar) primarily to feed the area's Jewish poor, this kosher kitchen was busiest during the Great Depression, when it provided meals to more than 5,000 people each week.

Walk to the end of Brune Street and turn left into Toynbee Street. Cross Toynbee and follow it around to the right onto Commercial Street. Cross Commercial and turn left. Then walk 1 block to:

13. **Christ Church Spitalfields** (☎ 0171/247-7202), built
between 1714 and 1729. The masterpiece of architect
Nicholas Hawksmoor, it originally served Huguenot refugees. A glance at the many 18th-century gravestones re-
veals that a majority bear French names.

   Leave the church and turn right onto Commercial Street;
cross Fournier Street, passing the Ten Bells Public House,
and take the first right into Puma Court. Midway on the
left side are the almshouses (dating from 1860) intended to
provide housing for the neighborhood poor. At the end of
Puma Court, turn left into Wilkes Street, and then turn
right into Princelet Street. On the left is the:

14. **Site of the first Yiddish theater in England.** Founded
in 1862, the Hebrew Amateur Society often drew record
crowds. Jacob Adler, one of the best-known actors of his
time, often appeared here. On January 18, 1887, a false cry
of "Fire!" during a performance caused a stampede that left
17 people crushed to death. Shortly thereafter, Adler and
his troupe emigrated to New York City, where he was influential in founding the American Yiddish Theater, which
had a great impact not only on American theater but also
on the Hollywood film industry.

   One block farther along Princelet Street, on the left,
is the:

15. **Heritage Centre,** 19 Princelet St. At first this was a series
of weavers' homes with large attic windows. Look for the
old weaver's symbol above the building's front door. In 1862,
this center became a Liberal Jewish meeting place and house
of worship called the Chevra Hidrath Chem. In 1870, the
Chevra bought the back garden of the house and built the
United Friends Synagogue. Though the building no longer
functions as a synagogue, it's the third-oldest synagogue still
standing in London and much of the interior is still intact.

   Proceed another block along Princelet Street and turn
left onto Brick Lane. Pause at the next corner (Hanbury
Street) to look at the building across the street; it's the former
site of the:

16. **Truman Black Eagle Brewery.** By the late 17th century, brewing was emerging from its small-scale operation
into a large commercial enterprise. The East End was

favored by the new, larger breweries because clean, fresh water was readily available and the odors arising from the brewing process could dissipate out over open fields.

The Black Eagle Brewery was founded on this site in 1666 by Joseph Truman. Over the centuries the brewery grew; by the 19th century it had become the world's largest brewery, claiming to be able to float a battleship on 1 year's production alone. The brewery closed in the 1980s, and the future use of this site has yet to be determined.

Turn right into Hanbury Street and stay on the right side. After 3 blocks, turn right into Spelman Street. The first building on the right is the:

Take a Break **Alma Tavern,** 41 Spelman St. (☎ **0171/247-5604**). This pub was opened in 1854 by Edmund Tilney, a soldier who had just returned to London from service in the Crimean War. He named it after the only allied victory there—the battle of the Alma. One of the few true "local pubs" remaining in London, it's owned by Steve Kane, who will happily allow you behind the bar to have your photo taken pulling a pint. Home-cooked lunches are available between noon and 2pm.

In the pub's back room, you'll find a:

17. **Jack the Ripper Exhibition,** commemorating the series of murders that took place in this neighborhood over a 12-week period during the fall of 1888. Five prostitutes were murdered and their bodies horribly mutilated. Although no one was ever charged with these crimes, many conjectures have been made about the criminal's identity. This exhibit depicts numerous suspects, as well as the victims and the police officers who investigated the crime.

Exit the Alma and go immediately right to Princelet Street. Two blocks later turn left onto Brick Lane. Walk 1 block, and on your right will be the:

18. **Great Mosque Spitalfields.** This building, more than any other in the neighborhood, reflects the area's changing demographics. Built in 1742 as a Huguenot chapel, it was acquired 50 years later by the London Society, a group dedicated to converting Jews to Christianity. It offered £50 to any proselyte who agreed to resettle in a Christian district. By 1892, however, when it issued its final report, the

society acknowledged that it had made only 16 bona-fide converts. The building then became a Methodist chapel, was later converted into the Great Synagogue Spitalfields, and in 1976 was sold to the Bangladeshi community, which converted it to a mosque.

Stroll along Fournier Street, where the houses were built specifically for the Huguenot refugees who had fled France after the revocation of the Edict of Nantes in 1685. Since many of the refugees were skillful weavers, the houses were designed with large attic windows to provide as much daylight as possible for them to work at their looms. Many of the houses have now been beautifully restored.

Backtrack to Brick Lane, turn right, and then turn right again into:

19. **Fashion Street.** At one time or another this street has been home to several well-known writers, including playwright Arnold Wesker and Hollywood screenwriter Wolf Mankowitz. Another resident was Israel Zangwill, whose first novel, *Children of the Ghetto,* was published in 1892, while he was teaching at a local Jewish school. Zangwill's phonetic translations of Yiddish East End speech angered the school authorities, who were trying to teach correct English, and he was obliged to resign from his teaching position. However, he later became the first secretary of the World Zionist Federation.

Jack London's reputation was already established when he took up residence here in 1902. He had come to England for the coronation of Edward VII but was dismayed to observe the contrast between the opulence of the event and the dire poverty of so many Londoners. Wanting to experience firsthand the hardships of the impoverished, he decided to live in the East End. He recorded his experiences in *The People of the Abyss.*

Backtrack to Brick Lane and turn right. Walk straight ahead until you reach the traffic lights, then turn left onto Whitechapel Road. Six blocks later, cross the street at the pedestrian walkway. To your left is the:

20. **Whitechapel Bell Foundry,** 324 Whitechapel Rd. (☎ 0171/247-2544), which has been casting bells since 1570 (but only at this location since 1783). Some of the

world's most famous bells have been cast here, including Big Ben, Westminster Abbey's, and America's original Liberty Bell.

Retrace your footsteps but stay on the left side of Whitechapel Road for 2 blocks. Cross Adler Street; on the left is a grassy area, the former site of:

21. **St. Mary's Church,** a 13th-century structure destroyed by bombs during World War II. It had been a common procedure to limewash the exteriors of important buildings; St. Mary's was the "White Chapel" that imparted its name to the entire area.

Proceed along Whitechapel Road, cross Whitechapel at the traffic lights, and then cross Brick Lane. The street now becomes Whitechapel High Street; half a block ahead on your right is the:

22. **Whitechapel Public Library.** This was once the hub of London's Jewish intellectual community, a group that included humanist Jacob Bronowsky, mathematician Selig Brodetsky, poet Isaac Rosenberg, and novelist Israel Zangwill. These men, and others, met almost daily in the reference reading room, where they exchanged ideas and debated intensely.

Next door is the:

23. **Whitechapel Art Gallery,** 80 Whitechapel High St. (☎ **0171/377-0107**). Built between 1897 and 1899, the gallery is housed in an unusual art nouveau building designed by C. H. Townsend. Founded by Canon Samuel Barnet, a local Jewish intellectual, the gallery originally displayed the works of the local impressionist painter Mark Gertler. A lively lecture series attracted such luminaries as George Bernard Shaw. Today, some of the world's best modern art is often exhibited.

Continue walking along Whitechapel High Street to arrive at Aldgate East Underground Station.

Clerkenwell

Start: Barbican Underground Station.

Finish: Farringdon Underground Station.

Time: 2 hours.

Best Time: Weekends, when less traffic permits a more pleasant stroll.

Worst Time: None.

London's "hidden village," Clerkenwell is a quirky little quarter, nestled between Bloomsbury and the City. Its heyday came in the 17th century, when upper-class people built stately homes near the water well for which this area was named. Whether we realize it or not, however, most of us know the Clerkenwell of the 19th century because this was the stomping grounds of Charles Dickens, and many of the sights, smells, and sounds described in his novels he undoubtedly experienced on these streets. During those years, the area was highly industrialized, densely populated, and tragically poor. It has since been revitalized, but many of the Georgian and Victorian buildings still hint at Clerkenwell's colorful history.

• • • • • • • • • • • • • • • •

Exit Barbican Underground Station and turn left onto Aldersgate Street. Take the first left into Carthusian Street and walk 1 block on the right to:

1. **Charterhouse Square,** a 14th-century burial pit. A number of catastrophes have befallen London over the years, but few have been as devastating as the bubonic plague—Black Death—that killed thousands in 1348. Churchyards, the traditional burial grounds of the time, couldn't cope with the overwhelming number of deaths, so plague pits for mass burials were dug in several open spaces around London. Charterhouse Square is the site of one such pit, located just on the other side of this fence. The pit, which originally covered 13 acres, was donated to the City in 1350 by Sir Walter de Manny, a knight who sympathized with victims of the Black Death. Although chronicler John Stow later claimed that 50,000 people were buried here, most historians don't believe that London's entire population at the time exceeded 35,000.

    With the fence on your left, enter Charterhouse Square, walking past:

2. **Florin Court,** the art deco building on your right. This was the site of the apartment of Agatha Christie's Belgian detective Hercule Poirot, he of the "little gray cells." You may recognize the building if you're a fan of the Poirot TV series starring David Suchet.

    Follow the fence around, then turn right through the huge wooden doors of the:

3. **Charterhouse** (☎ 0171/253-9503), a retirement home for men who've served in the armed forces. The house was founded by Sir Walter de Manny in 1370 as a monastery for Carthusian monks. Built by Henry Yevele, Edward III's master mason, the house enabled the monks to live in solitude 6 days a week. On Sunday, however, they came together in the refectory for their meal, then were allowed a 3-hour outdoor recess that was the only time they were permitted to talk to one another.

    In 1535, the monastery's prior, John Houghton, invited Thomas Cromwell, then Henry VIII's vicar general, to a discussion on the king's supremacy as head of the English church. Cromwell responded by arranging for the monks to be imprisoned and tried for "treacherously machinating and desiring to deprive the King of his title as supreme head of the church." After his conviction, Houghton was hung, drawn, and quartered. As a warning to others, one of his arms was nailed onto the monastery's entrance gate.

The monastery surrendered to the king in 1537 and eventually came into the possession of John Dudley, duke of Northumberland. Dudley may have used the Charterhouse as a residence for his son, Guilford Dudley, and Guilford's wife, Lady Jane Grey, who in July 1553 was proclaimed queen on the death of Edward VI. (Afraid that Edward's Roman Catholic sister, Mary, would turn Protestant England Catholic if she became queen, John Dudley persuaded the young king to name Jane his successor.) However, she was queen for only 9 days: Once Mary's claim to the throne was recognized, Jane and her husband were tried for high treason and then beheaded. This story may sound familiar if you've seen the movie *Lady Jane* starring Helena Bonham Carter and Cary Elwes.

The Charterhouse was purchased in 1611 (for £13,000, a handsome sum at the time) by Thomas Sutton, who wanted the home to serve as a school for poor boys and a retirement home for men. Until 1892, the school successfully educated thousands of disadvantaged Londoners, including Baron Baden-Powell, founder of the Scouts movement; author William Makepeace Thackeray; and John Wesley, founder of the Methodist Church.

Guided tours leave from the main gate Wednesdays at 2:15pm from April to July.

Exit the Charterhouse, turn right, and continue through the iron gates to Charterhouse Street. On the right is the:

Take a Break   **Fox and Anchor Public House,** 116 Charterhouse St. (☎ **0171/253-4838**). By law, London pubs are allowed to open Monday to Saturday from 11am to 11pm and Sunday from noon to 10:30pm. But the Fox and Anchor is an exception. Known locally as an "early house," this tavern is specially licensed to serve alcohol between 6:30 and 9:30am, enabling it to accommodate the early-morning workers at Smithfield Market, London's primary meat market. If you're taking this tour early in the

Clerkenwell

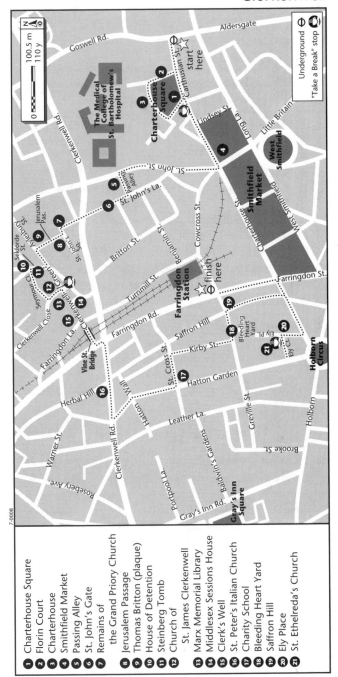

1. Charterhouse Square
2. Florin Court
3. Charterhouse
4. Smithfield Market
5. Passing Alley
6. St. John's Gate
7. Remains of
   the Grand Priory Church
8. Jerusalem Passage
9. Thomas Britton (plaque)
10. House of Detention
11. Steinberg Tomb
12. Church of
    – St. James Clerkenwell
13. Marx Memorial Library
14. Middlesex Sessions House
15. Clerk's Well
16. St. Peter's Italian Church
17. Charity School
18. Bleeding Heart Yard
19. Saffron Hill
20. Ely Place
21. St. Ethelreda's Church

day, stop here for one of the pub's world-famous English breakfasts.

Exit the pub and turn right along Charterhouse Street. Half a block farther, the large building you'll see on the opposite side of the street is:

4. **Smithfield Market,** formerly the "smoothfield"—a grassy area just outside the City gates, where a weekly horse fair was held during the Middle Ages. In 1638, the City Corporation established a cattle market here. As the city expanded, encircling the market, residents complained about the general filth and the drunken behavior of market workers. So in 1855 the livestock market was moved to Islington.

With the market on your left, continue 1 block down Charterhouse Street and turn right onto St. John Street. Cross to the left side and walk 2 blocks (past the White Bear Pub), turning left into the small covered passageway called:

5. **Passing Alley,** a small alleyway that served as a public toilet before modern sanitation measures were adopted. Before the advent of indoor plumbing, London sported a whole network of back alleys for pubgoers. This one was originally called Pissing Alley, and its name was changed only in the last century.

At the end of Passing Alley, turn right onto St. John's Lane and walk just a few steps to:

6. **St. John's Gate,** St. John's Lane (☎ 0171/253-6644). Once the main entrance to the 12th-century Priory of the Knights Hospitallers of St. John of Jerusalem, it's the only monastic gatehouse left in London. The priory no longer exists, but the gateway, dating from 1504, has served a variety of functions.

During the reign of Henry VIII (1509–47), the gatehouse was used as office space for the king's administrators. From 1731 to 1781 it was the headquarters of *Gentleman's Magazine,* a popular periodical whose contributors included Oliver Goldsmith and Samuel Johnson. Johnson was given a special room in which to write; it's said that he literally locked himself away so that no one could get in and tempt him out or disturb him.

In subsequent years, the gatehouse was turned into the parish watch house; later, it became the Old Jerusalem Tavern. In 1874, it became the property of the Most Venerable Order of the Hospital of St. John of Jerusalem, a Protestant order founded in 1831 to uphold the traditions of the medieval hospitallers. It was here that the St. John's Ambulance Brigade, one of the world's first, was founded in 1877.

Today the gatehouse serves as a museum and library. Tours are offered on Tuesday, Friday, and Saturday at 11am and 2:30pm. There's an admission charge.

Walk through the gate and continue straight ahead, across busy Clerkenwell Road. Proceed into St. John's Square. The iron gates on your right guard the:

7. **Remains of the Grand Priory Church,** the 12th-century church for which the gatehouse was the main entrance. All of the monastic foundations, which flourished in medieval times, were secularized by Henry VIII in 1540, leaving few traces behind. The remains of this church, just north of the old City walls, are some of the best-preserved examples of those monasteries.

   With your back to the church gates, bear right into:

8. **Jerusalem Passage,** a small thoroughfare that was once the site of the priory's northern gate. It's an attractive street that flourished in the last century with small shops and boutiques. Most of the structures you see here today were erected on medieval foundations.

   At the end of the short passage, high up on your right, is a green wall plaque commemorating:

9. **Thomas Britton** (1644–1714), a local coal merchant and lover of music. Knowledgeable in chemistry, a respected collector of rare books, and a talented musician, Britton was widely known as the "Musical Coalman." A sort of Renaissance man, he established an informal music club that met above his rather dingy shop, formerly located on this site. The club attracted celebrated musicians of the day as well as members of the royal court.

   Turn left onto Aylesbury Street, then take the first right onto Sekforde Street. Stay to the left and follow the road left into St. James's Walk. Turn left into Sans Walk and then take the first right into the unnamed alleyway where, a little way along on the right, is the:

10. **House of Detention** (☎ 0171/253-9494). Sealed up in 1890, this building was recently reopened; it's one of London's most interesting underground experiences. You're escorted into an underground prison complex by your own special guide. The tour begins on the "Dark Walk," which provided the ventilation for some 10,000 remand prisoners who were incarcerated here each year. Then you're taken by a uniformed prison guard along granite passages, past dank, dark dungeons toward a group of prison cells where an interesting exhibit is displayed.

   Many prisoners who were shipped off to the New World in the 18th century spent their last days here. When America decided that it no longer wanted England's criminals, they were sent instead to Botany Bay in Australia.

   Backtrack to Sans Walk and turn right. Stay to the left side and enter Clerkenwell Close. Follow this around as it bears left twice; after 2 blocks, turn left through the gates into the gardens of St. James's Church. Straight ahead, to the right of the second set of steps, is the:

11. **Steinberg Tomb,** the grave of a murdered family. The Steinberg murders horrified the country when they occurred in 1834. Although the stone's inscription has worn away, you can still make out the name Steinberg—the surname of Ellen and her four young children, who were stabbed to death on September 8 by their husband and father, John Nicholas Steinberg, before he turned the knife on himself. Londoners were so distressed by the murders that they took up a collection to have Ellen and her children interred here.

   Since the murderer committed suicide, he couldn't be buried in a churchyard. Outraged citizens took Steinberg's coffin to a pauper's graveyard on nearby Ray Street. The burial took place at night; tipped from the coffin directly into the grave, the corpse was struck over the head with an iron mallet and a stake was driven through his heart.

   Backtrack toward Clerkenwell Close. Just before you reach the gates is the:

12. **Church of St. James Clerkenwell,** Clerkenwell Gardens. The original 1568 church was once a part of a

Benedictine nunnery dedicated to St. Mary. Rebuilt in 1792 to include an elegant Wren-style steeple, it became independent after the nunnery closed in 1849. Inside you can see several monuments from the original church; if the building is open, it's worth a look.

Exit onto Clerkenwell Close and proceed ahead onto Clerkenwell Green; on the corner you'll find the:

☕ **Take a Break** **Crown Tavern,** 43 Clerkenwell Green (☎ **0171/250-0757**). Established in 1641 and rebuilt in 1815, the Crown gained fame in the 19th century because of its Apollo Concert Room, a live-music hall that was open every evening. The downstairs room of this bilevel pub still displays Victorian-era playbills. Today, the only entertainment is conversation among the patrons. A good selection of food and drink is always available.

In the main bar you can still open and close the "snob screens"—screens that were placed here long ago to separate those who belonged to the working class from those of the middle class (who were in a "private" bar).

Exit the tavern and cross Clerkenwell Close; three doors along on the right will bring you to the:

13. **Marx Memorial Library,** 37A Clerkenwell Green (☎ **0171/253-1485**). Though this building dates from 1738, it acquired its present designation in 1933—the 50th anniversary of Karl Marx's death. The library, which houses more than 100,000 books and periodicals, is open most afternoons; you can see the Lenin room (where he edited *Iskra* in 1902 and 1903).

Continue along Clerkenwell Green. The large building opposite is the:

14. **Middlesex Sessions House,** a former courthouse built in 1779 by architect John Rogers. The stone reliefs adorning the front facade represent Justice and Mercy. By 1919, London's expanding criminal population had outgrown this building, and when the courts moved, the house was converted into offices. In 1979, the building was acquired by the Masonic Foundation and restored to its former glory.

Continue walking along the right side of Clerkenwell Green. At the end, turn right into Farringdon Lane. A few doors along on the right is the:

15. **Clerk's Well,** 16 Farringdon Lane, the water supply that gave the area its name. Peer through the windows of the building that now stands on this site to see the remains of this well. St. Mary's Nunnery, located nearby, drew water from this well, which was known as the "Fons Clericorum" (clerk's well).

Backtrack along Farringdon Lane and take the first right into Vine Street Bridge. Cross over Farringdon Road at the traffic lights and proceed into Clerkenwell Road. A few doors along on the right is:

16. **St. Peter's Italian Church** (☎ 0171/837-1528), designed by J. M. Brydon and opened in 1863 to serve the large Italian population of the area, known at the time as Little Italy. The church has a strong musical tradition, and in the 19th and early 20th century Italian opera singers like Enrico Caruso often sang at mass here. To view the church's magnificent interior, call the number above.

Exit the church and cautiously cross Clerkenwell Road to take the first left into Hatton Garden, which has been the center of London's jewelry trade since 1836. Three blocks farther, at the corner of St. Cross Street, is the former:

17. **Charity School,** designed by Sir Christopher Wren. It was originally a small chapel intended to serve the spiritual needs of the neighborhood, but later it became a charity school. Above the door are figures depicting the students of that time. The girl on the right holds in one hand a parchment, on which is written the cost of her expenses, while her other hand is outstretched to encourage passersby to make a contribution. The building is now used for offices.

Continue along St. Cross Street and make the first right into Kirby Street. At its end, turn left into Greville Street. The first turn on your right is:

18. **Bleeding Heart Yard.** In 1576, early in her reign, Elizabeth I decided to deed this land to her friend Sir Christopher Hatton. The only problem was that she didn't own the land; it belonged to the Bishop of Ely. When the queen asked him to relinquish it, he refused, prompting the queen to write: "Proud Prelate, remember what thou werst before we made thee. Comply, or by God we shall defrock thee." And so the bishop complied.

Popular myth has it that Sir Christopher's wife, Lady Hatton, entered into a pact with the devil. One evening, in the midst of a party here, the devil appeared and took Lady Hatton away. According to the legend:

" . . . out in the courtyard, and just in that part where the pump stands—lay bleeding a large human heart."

The pump is no longer here, nor for that matter is the heart, but the yard name commerates the devilish pact.

Exit Bleeding Heart Yard, continue 1 block along Greville Street, and then turn right into:

19. **Saffron Hill,** named for the spice that was once sold here. In the 18th century, this area was part of the gardens of the Bishop of Ely. Saffron was popular in the days before refrigeration because of its ability to disguise the taste of rancid meat.

By the 19th century, Saffron Hill had become a notorious criminal rookery. Theft was so common it was said that you could have your handkerchief stolen at one end of the street and buy it back at the other! In *Oliver Twist,* Charles Dickens referred to Saffron Hill, calling it Field Court, the place where Fagin had his lair and where young children were trained in the art of pickpocketing.

At the end of Saffron Hill, go up the steps and turn right. Half a block farther, go through the gates into:

20. **Ely Place,** former site of the palace of the Bishops of Ely, until Elizabeth I demanded that the land be given to Sir Christopher Hatton. The 19 charming houses that now stand here comprise London's most perfectly preserved Georgian precinct. Until recently, Ely Place was controlled by the Council of Cambridgeshire, not London. Consequently, the Metropolitan Police had no jurisdiction here and couldn't enter or arrest any suspect who walked through the gates on your right. The property is protected by beadles, private guards with authority to eject anyone who causes a disturbance. As you enter the gates you pass the beadles hut, with its white chimney.

Farther inside the courtyard, hidden away on your left, is:

21. **St. Etheldreda's Church,** Ely Place. Built at the end of the 13th century, the church was named for St. Etheldreda (St. Awdry), an abbess who died in A.D. 679 from a throat tumor that was said to have been inflicted on her as punishment for her fondness for beaded necklaces. The type of devotional beads she wore (which were of cheap quality) came to be known as St. Awdrys, which was shortened to tawdrys—a word still in use today.

Enter the church, which is best known for its ancient crypt and spectacular postwar stained glass. The arches of the crypt, dating from 1251, architecturally combine Norman and Gothic styles.

Exit the church and return to Ely Place. Turn right at Ely Court. On your right you'll arrive at:

Take a Break **Ye Olde Mitre Tavern,** 1 Ely Court (☎ 0171/405-4751). Built in 1546 for the servants of the Bishop of Ely, this beautiful Elizabethan pub was known to Samuel Johnson, Charles Dickens, and other famous local wordsmiths. Before you enter, look at the cherry tree that's now preserved behind glass by the front door. This tree used to be the boundary marker between the land the Bishop of Ely was allowed to keep and the land he was compelled to give Sir Christopher Hatton (in return for one red rose a year). The Mitre Tavern offers a good selection of real ales and is justifiably famous for its toasted sandwiches.

Exit the Tavern, backtrack to Ely Place, and turn right. At Charterhouse Street, turn left and left again on Farringdon Road. One block along, turn right into Cowcross Street to arrive at Farringdon Underground Station.

Bloomsbury

Start: Holborn Underground Station.

Finish: Holborn Underground Station.

Time: 1½ hours.

Best Time: Monday to Saturday during daylight hours.

Worst Time: At night and on Sunday (when the pubs are closed).

Bloomsbury's convenient location, just north of Soho and west of the City, has been a significant factor in its development and charm. And its close proximity to businesses, shops, and theaters has long made this area a desirable place to live. Several large hotels and dozens of smaller B&Bs testify to Bloomsbury's equal appeal to visitors.

Bloomsbury dates from the late 17th century; it was laid out around a series of squares that helped promote the area as London's newest social center. In the early 20th century, it gained fame for its large concentration of important writers and thinkers, including Clive and Vanessa Bell, E. M. Forster, Lytton Strachey, Bertrand Russell, John Maynard Keynes, and Leonard and Virginia Woolf—who collectively became known as the Bloomsbury Group.

The class system is still quite evident in Bloomsbury, where most of the land is still owned by a single person—the earl of Bedford. The two largest occupants, however, are the British

Museum and the University of London, which keep the area alive with new faces and ideas. Bloomsbury has developed into a curious mix of private residences and public institutions—a well-balanced combination that seems to benefit everyone. For you, this means beautifully tended streets, historically significant buildings, interesting residents, and several major attractions.

• • • • • • • • • • • • • • • •

Leave Holborn Underground Station, cross High Holborn at the traffic light, and turn left. One block later, turn right into Southampton Place, an 18th-century street named after the 1st earl of Southampton. Several well-preserved Georgian houses from the 1740s line this block. On your left is:

1. **17 Southampton Place,** the former home of John Henry, Cardinal Newman (1801–90). An eminent theologian, Newman became a leading member of the ill-fated Oxford movement, an attempt to return England's Protestant Anglican Church to its traditional heritage. He failed to persuade England's relatively progressive clergy that this approach was desirable, but his Oxfords, named for the university where the movement was based, went so far back to their religious roots that Newman became Roman Catholic!

   Continue along Southampton Place to turn left and walk clockwise around Bloomsbury Square. The first house on the square to your left, just after the traffic lights, is:

2. **6 Bloomsbury Square,** the former home of Isaac D'Israeli (1766–1848), author and father of the Victorian-era prime minister Benjamin Disraeli (who changed the spelling of his surname). Isaac was born in England to Sephardic Jews who had fled from persecution in Spain. Educated in Amsterdam, he was both an intellectual and a respected writer. The older D'Israeli's literary works include *Curiosities of Literature* (1791), a volume of anecdotes and essays that went into 12 editions.

   Continue around the square to:

3. **20 Bloomsbury Square,** the former home of Gertrude Stein (1874–1946) and her brother, Leo. The Steins rented

Bloomsbury

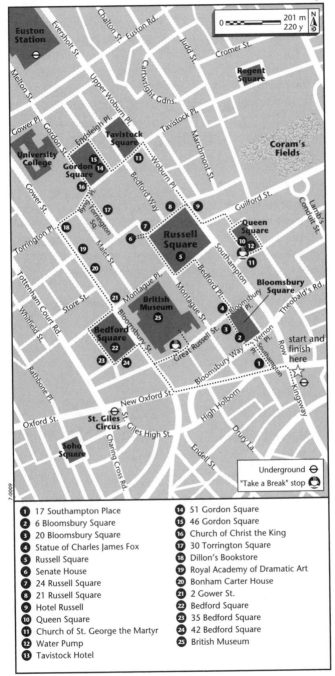

1. 17 Southampton Place
2. 6 Bloomsbury Square
3. 20 Bloomsbury Square
4. Statue of Charles James Fox
5. Russell Square
6. Senate House
7. 24 Russell Square
8. 21 Russell Square
9. Hotel Russell
10. Queen Square
11. Church of St. George the Martyr
12. Water Pump
13. Tavistock Hotel
14. 51 Gordon Square
15. 46 Gordon Square
16. Church of Christ the King
17. 30 Torrington Square
18. Dillon's Bookstore
19. Royal Academy of Dramatic Art
20. Bonham Carter House
21. 2 Gower St.
22. Bedford Square
23. 35 Bedford Square
24. 42 Bedford Square
25. British Museum

an apartment here in 1902, after Gertrude failed to get her medical degree at Johns Hopkins University in Baltimore. A voracious reader and writer, Gertrude enjoyed living near the British Museum's Reading Room, where she immersed herself in the works of novelist Anthony Trollope. But Stein complained of London's depressing grayness; after spending a year on Bloomsbury Square, she left for Paris, the city that would become her adopted home. There she lived with Alice B. Toklas.

Keeping the gardens to your right, walk a few steps farther and pause at the:

4. **Statue of Charles James Fox,** 18th-century leader of the Whigs in the House of Commons. Plump and convivial, Fox (1749–1806) had an enormous appetite for both food and drink. His charisma and oratorical talent established him as England's leading radical. He opposed war with America and expressed sympathy toward the French Revolution. George III profoundly distrusted him, yet the Prince of Wales (later George IV) was his close friend. The statue depicts Fox as a champion of English freedom—a toga-clad Consul holding a copy of the Magna Carta, with the seal faithfully copied from the original in the British Museum.

With your back to the statue, cross the road and go straight ahead into Bedford Place, a street that ends at:

5. **Russell Square.** Because of its proximity to museums, hotels, and the Underground Station, this square has become the de facto center of Bloomsbury. Constructed in 1800, it's named after the Russell family, headed by the earl of Bedford, one of London's largest landowners. Because of its beauty and excellent location—close to both the City and the West End—Russell Square and the surrounding area has always been popular with lawyers, physicians, and other well-to-do professionals.

In the gardens is a **statue of Francis Russell,** 5th duke of Bedford (1765–1802), who oversaw the development of much of Bloomsbury on the former site of his family's ancestral home, Bedford House. Because the duke served on the first Board of Agriculture and helped develop modern methods of farming, the statue depicts him with one hand resting on a plough and the other holding a sheaf of corn.

Turn left onto the square and walk 1 block; at the pedestrian crossing, cross over toward the gardens. Continue straight ahead until you come to the next pedestrian crossing; there turn left and cross the road. Go right for half a block, then turn left through the gates to the courtyard of:

6. **Senate House,** designed by Charles Holden and completed in 1937. Known locally as the "Big House in Bloomsbury," it's now the administration building of the University of London.

   During World War II, it housed the Ministry of Information, where journalists would come for official news releases about the war. Graham Greene, who worked here, described it as "a beacon guiding the German planes toward King's Cross and St. Pancras Stations. . . . I wrote a letter to the *Spectator* with the title 'Bloomsbury Lighthouse' [after which] the lights were dimmed."

   George Orwell modeled his Ministry of Truth (Minitrue in Newspeak) after this building in his *Nineteen Eighty-four*. As he described it, "The Ministry of Truth . . . was startlingly different from any other object in sight. It was an enormous pyramidical structure of glittering white concrete, soaring up, terrace after terrace, three hundred metres into the air. . . . It was too strong, it could not be stormed. A thousand rocket bombs would not batter it down."

   Backtrack to the gates and turn left onto Russell Square. Continue walking clockwise around the square until you reach:

7. **24 Russell Square,** where poet T. S. Eliot worked as a book publisher with the firm Faber and Faber. In addition to being a successful writer, Eliot was a prosperous businessman. In his time, as well as today, a rich writer was something of an anomaly. Eliot was generous to his less well-to-do friends. In his diary, fellow writer Roy Campbell (1902–57) related that when he and Dylan Thomas were in need of money, they called on "his grace" (Eliot) and were rewarded lavishly.

   Just a few doors ahead, along Russell Square, you'll see:

8. **21 Russell Square,** the former home of Sir Samuel Romilly (1757–1818). A lawyer and legal reformer, Romilly is best remembered for his success in reducing England's

large number of offenses that were punishable by death. Romilly's own beliefs were clearly shaped by his Huguenot background. His influence on English politics and policies shouldn't be underestimated. Along with his friend and confidant abolitionist William Wilberforce, Romilly played a significant role in stopping Britain's slave trade in the Caribbean and elsewhere.

Two blocks ahead, at the corner of Southampton Row, is the ornate:

9. **Hotel Russell,** perhaps the most beautiful building in Bloomsbury, opened in 1900. The hotel's ornate facade is one of the finest examples of late Victorian Renaissance architecture in London and somewhat resembles the Houses of Parliament building and nearby St. Pancras train station. Prospective guests might want to know that, alas, the interior (consisting of some 300 rooms) isn't as elegant. Still, it's worth a look.

The Russell is on the site of the former Pankhurst home. England's most famous suffragettes, Emmeline Pankhurst and her daughters, Christabel and Sylvia, lived here from 1888 to 1893; during the first decade of the 20th century, the Pankhurst sisters led the fight in England for women's right to vote and other forms of enfranchisement.

Continue around Russell Square and turn left after the hotel onto Guilford Street. Take your first right down a narrow passageway, Queen Anne's Walk, to enter:

10. **Queen Square,** a pretty plaza that was laid out in the early 18th century and named after Queen Anne. Once a fancy residential square, the green is now surrounded by hospitals and is a popular lunching spot for local workers.

Walk counterclockwise around the square. One block ahead, on your right, you'll see the:

Take a Break **Queen's Larder,** 1 Queen Square (☎ 0171/837-5627). This comfortable tavern serves good food and drink but deserves special mention for its unusual history. When George III became mentally ill, he took up residence nearby, at the home of his attending physician, Dr. Willis. In order to help her husband, Queen Charlotte rented cellar space beneath this building to store some of her husband's favorite foods. This pub, Queen's

Larder (which means "pantry"), opened later in George III's reign.

Directly across the street from the pub is the:

11. **Church of St. George the Martyr** (1706), sometimes referred to as the "sweeps church." In the 18th and 19th centuries, poor boys—usually about 8 to 10 years old—often worked to clean chimneys using their small bodies as brushes. Sympathizing with the plight of these impoverished youngsters, a local resident, Capt. James South, established a charity at this church to help them.

Cross the street to the square's inside sidewalk and continue walking counterclockwise around the square. On the south side of the square, pause at the:

12. **Water Pump.** This iron pump, dating from the early 1900s, commemorates the fact that Queen Square was once a water reservoir for the surrounding community. Times have changed, however, and the pump now carries a warning: "Unfit for drinking."

Continue around the square, step inside the gardens if you wish, then backtrack to the Russell. With the hotel on your right, walk 2 long blocks up Woburn Place to Tavistock Square. Turn left on Tavistock Square and stop outside the:

13. **Tavistock Hotel,** a large building that occupies the site of the former home of Leonard and Virginia Woolf. The Woolfs moved here in March 1929 and remained in Bloomsbury for 15 years. Virginia wrote in a large upstairs room that was illuminated by a skylight. The building's basement housed Hogarth Press, a publishing house that issued books by Woolf and T. S. Eliot as well as English translations of the works of Sigmund Freud. Virginia left this house just 19 months before she drowned herself in the River Ouse.

Continue along Tavistock Square, cross Bedford Way, and enter Gordon Square. After 1 block, turn right. Soon you'll come to:

14. **51 Gordon Square,** the former home of Lytton Strachey (1880–1932). Strachey, a seminal writer and thinker, was an antiwar activist and conscientious objector during World War I. His well-regarded book *Eminent Victorians* is widely

viewed as the first biographical novel—a new literary genre that mixed fact and fiction. When Strachey bought this house in 1919, he wrote to Virginia Woolf, "Very soon I foresee that the whole Square will become a sort of college, and *rencontres* in the garden I shudder to think of."

Next door, a plaque on the wall of no. 50 commemorates the **Bloomsbury Group,** London's most famous circle of writers, artists, and musicians in the early 20th century. Singing, dancing, reading, debating, and a fair amount of debauchery brought publicity to the group's regular soirées. But not everyone was impressed by the events and antics of the Bloomsbury Group. Gertrude Stein dismissed them contemptuously as the "Young Men's Christian Association—with Christ left out."

Continue along for three doors to arrive at:

15. **46 Gordon Square,** the former home of John Maynard Keynes (1883–1946). An eminent economist, Keynes played a leading role in the negotiations that led to the establishment of the International Monetary Fund, one of the world's most significant economic bodies. Keynes turned his home into a meeting place for Bloomsbury's creative community. The gatherings were often attended by Virginia Woolf and Lytton Strachey as well as ballerina Lydia Lopokova (who later married Keynes).

With your back to no. 45, cross over and enter the gardens (open Mon–Fri 8am–8pm). If they're locked, walk around to the opposite side. Cross the road and turn left. One half block ahead on Gordon Square (on the right) is the:

16. **Church of Christ the King,** designed by Raphael Brandon in 1853 and widely considered the finest mid-Victorian church in London. Now used by the University of London, it was originally a Catholic Apostolic Church. It boasts exquisite stained-glass windows.

Exit the church and turn right. Cross Byng Place and proceed ahead to pass through the barrier into Torrington Square. A short way down on the left is:

17. **30 Torrington Square,** the former home of poet Christina Georgina Rossetti (1830–94). When her most famous narrative poem, "Goblin Market," published in

1861, brought her fame, she was too shy to participate in the literary social gatherings of her day. She never married and was significantly influenced by her brother, Dante Gabriel Rossetti, the poet and painter.

Together with her mother, Christina moved to this house in 1876 to care for two elderly aunts. After the death of her mother, aunts, and brother, she published no more poetry, though the verses she wrote during those years were published after her death (1894).

Backtrack to Byng Place and turn left. Cross Malet Street to:

18. **Dillon's Bookstore,** 82 Gower St. (☎ **0171/636-1577**). Founded in 1937 by Una Dillon, who had no previous bookselling experience, Dillon's has expanded to become the official bookshop of the University of London and one of England's most famous booksellers. Eccentric poet Dame Edith Sitwell (1887–1964) was a regular patron of this shop and often gave impromptu readings to astonished customers. If it's not mobbed with students, the store is definitely worth a browse.

Exit the bookstore and turn left into Gower Street. About a dozen B&Bs line the right side of this street, making it popular with both students and visitors. Most of the buildings on the left side are affiliated with the University of London. Two blocks down on the left is the:

19. **Royal Academy of Dramatic Art,** 62–64 Gower St. (☎ **0171/636-7076**). Founded in 1904 by Sir Herbert Beerbohm Tree, the academy has since then provided comprehensive training for the professional theater. On the premises are three fully equipped theaters, and forthcoming productions are listed on the board outside. Former students include Peter O'Toole, Sir John Gielgud, and Sir Anthony Hopkins.

Continue walking down Gower Street; 1 block farther on the left is the:

20. **Bonham Carter House,** 52 Gower St., a former surgeon's house and operating room. It was here in December 1846 that the first general anesthetic was administered in England.

Three blocks ahead on your left is:

21. **2 Gower St.,** the former home of Dame Millicent Garrett Fawcett (1847–1929). She was one of England's most influential figures in the campaign for women's suffrage. Steadfastly opposed to militant tactics, Fawcett fought politically, rising to become the leader of the so-called constitutional wing of the suffrage movement.

    Immediately, cross Gower Street and enter:

22. **Bedford Square,** Bloomsbury's last remaining wholly Georgian square. Laid out in 1775, the streets around the square were originally privately owned; access was limited to residents and to those who had a legitimate reason to be in the area. Many of the square's pretty doorframes are made of Coade Stone, an artificial material known for its weather resistance. When the Coade Artificial Stone Manufactory was closed in 1840, the secret of the stone's composition was lost.

    Walk counterclockwise around the square and pause outside:

23. **35 Bedford Square,** the former home of Thomas Wakley (1795–1862). Wakley, a surgeon, founded *The Lancet,* England's most prestigious medical journal. He started the periodical in order to criticize medical malpractice and nepotism, an endeavor that involved him in numerous libel actions. While serving as coroner for the West Middlesex Hospital, Wakley often allowed Charles Dickens to attend his inquests, which provided Dickens with a lot of material for his novels.

    As you continue walking around the square, take note of the house at:

24. **42 Bedford Square.** This was once the home of writer Sir Anthony Hope Hawkins (1863–1933), who is probably best known for his novel *The Prisoner of Zenda.*

    Continue around Bedford Square, turn right onto Bloomsbury Street, then turn left onto Great Russell Street. The huge building on your left is the:

25. **British Museum** (☎ 0171/636-1555). With its unmatched collection of important finds from Egypt, Greece, Rome, Cyprus, Asia, and the Middle East, the British Museum merits its own full-day walking tour. The Rosetta Stone, whose discovery in the 19th century enabled

modern scholars to understand Egyptian hieroglyphics, is at the entrance to the Egyptian sculpture gallery. A frieze from the Parthenon, known as the Elgin Marbles, is the most famous portion of the museum's extensive collection of Greek antiquities; they were named for Lord Elgin, who took them from Athens. (The Greek government is suing to have these treasures returned, since they comprise an important part of Greece's cultural heritage.) Also on display are 1,000-year-old Mesopotamian jewelry, Babylonian astronomical instruments, and Assyrian artifacts. Other fascinating exhibits are the contents of several Egyptian tombs, with their bandaged mummies.

To the right of the museum's entrance, on the ground floor, are the **British Library Galleries.** Rotating thematic displays come from the library's collection of more than 8 million books. Included in the permanent exhibit is one of the two surviving copies of the Magna Carta (1215), Shakespeare's First Folio (1623), and a Gutenberg Bible (ca. 1453)—the first book printed with movable (hence, reusable) type. Autographed works by Bach, Mozart, and Handel are on display. You may be able to look into the **British Library Reading Room,** a hushed research room that was regularly used by Gandhi, Lenin, George Bernard Shaw, Virginia Woolf, and others. Karl Marx wrote *Das Kapital* here. The museum is open Monday to Saturday from 10am to 5pm and Sunday from 2:30 to 6pm.

Just opposite the museum is the:

Take a Break **Museum Tavern,** 49 Great Russell St. (☎ **0171/242-8987**). It was known as the "British Museum" until 1873, and its location, across from the more famous British Museum, guarantees a touristy clientele. Still, the pub remains a popular refuge for local poets and scholars, making it a good place to end your tour.

After leaving the tavern, retrace your steps to Bloomsbury Street and turn left. At New Oxford Street, turn left and keep walking until it turns into High Holborn, then cross to Holborn Underground Station.

Soho

Start: Leicester Square Underground Station.

Finish: Piccadilly Circus Underground Station.

Time: 2½ hours, not counting cafe stops.

Best Times: Monday to Saturday from 9am to sunset.

Worst Times: Sunday, when most of Soho's shops are closed, and after dark, when Leicester Gardens are closed.

Since the 17th century, Soho has been London's most cosmopolitan area. Although well known for its nightclubs, cinemas, theaters, and restaurants, Soho is more than just nightlife. It's a complex amalgam of the successive immigrant groups that've established restaurants and other businesses here over the last 300 years. For example, it contains England's largest Chinatown.

Strolling around Soho, you can readily find traces of the Victorian era adjacent to theaters from the 1930s, beatnik cafes from the 1950s, rock hangouts from the 1960s, pornography shops from the 1970s, boutiques from the 1980s, and dance clubs from last night. After all these years, Soho is still the best place in London to find a great hidden restaurant or a fabulous all-night club. And London's entertainment district is also the center of the country's film industry, for Twentieth Century Fox and Warner Brothers have offices here.

This walk will give you an excellent overview of all that Soho has to offer. After you become acquainted with the area, return and explore those places that seem especially interesting.

● ● ● ● ● ● ● ● ● ● ● ● ● ● ● ● ●

Leave Leicester Square Underground Station via the Leicester Square exit and walk straight ahead to:

1. **Leicester Square,** Soho's most famous piazza. Leicester ("*Les*-ter") Square was known as Lammas Fields until the 1630s, when it was inherited by the earl of Leicester, who built his mansion here. The house became an alternative Royal Court in 1717, when the Prince of Wales (the future George II) took refuge here to escape the wrath of his tyrannical father, George I. Ironically, George II also became cruel to *his* son, Prince Frederick, who decided to move to Leicester House in 1742.

From 1792 (when Leicester House was demolished) to the mid-19th century, this area became rather dilapidated. There was a short-lived renaissance in 1851, when geographer James Wyld erected a model of the earth in a dome-shaped building that occupied the entire square.

A member of Parliament, Albert Grant, purchased this land in 1874 and commissioned James Knowles to design a public garden that would surround a memorial to Shakespeare and the busts of four famous residents. Shortly thereafter, the London plane trees that now tower over the square were planted. In 1975 Leicester Square was permanently closed to traffic, and in 1990 the Westminster County Council had the square renovated.

At the center of Leicester Square is:

2. **Leicester Square Gardens.** This bucolic green is surrounded by an iron fence with a garden gate at each of the park's four corners. Each gate is named for a famous writer, artist, or scientist who lived in the immediate area and is marked with an appropriate statue.

The entrance closest to you is **Hogarth Gate,** named for satirical artist/illustrator William Hogarth, who lived at 30 Leicester Square from 1736 until his death in 1764. Trained as an engraver, Hogarth became popular for his biting portrayals of his contemporaries. While living on the

Soho

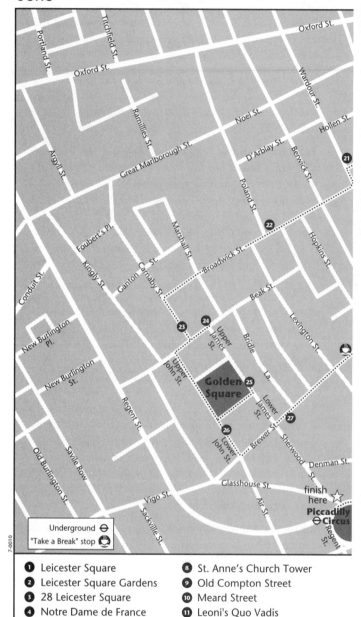

❶ Leicester Square	❽ St. Anne's Church Tower
❷ Leicester Square Gardens	❾ Old Compton Street
❸ 28 Leicester Square	❿ Meard Street
❹ Notre Dame de France	⓫ Leoni's Quo Vadis
❺ Lisle Street	⓬ Frith Street
❻ Polar Bear Pub	⓭ Wolfgang Amadeus
❼ Loon Fung Supermarket	Mozart House

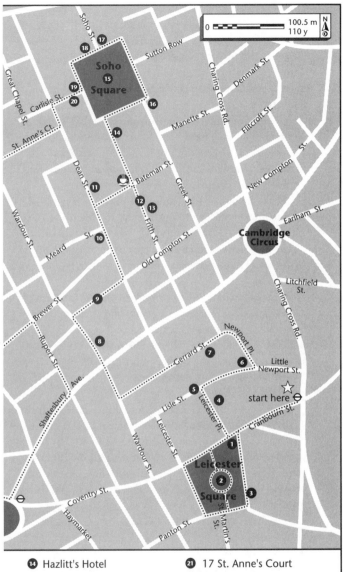

⑭ Hazlitt's Hotel	㉑ 17 St. Anne's Court
⑮ Soho Square	㉒ Broadwick Street Pump
⑯ House of St. Barnabus	㉓ Carnaby Street
⑰ 10 Soho Square	㉔ 41 Beak St.
⑱ French Protestant Church	㉕ 14 Golden Square
⑲ 2 Soho Square	㉖ 4 Lower John St.
⑳ Home of the earl of Carlisle	㉗ 71 Brewer St.

square (then known as Leicester Fields), Hogarth produced his most famous works, like *Marriage à la Mode, The Rake's Progress,* and *Industry and Idleness.* His illustrations were often pirated, which led Hogarth to campaign for passage of the Copyright Law of 1735 (otherwise known as Hogarth's Act).

Go to the center of the square to see the **statue of William Shakespeare.** The scroll in the statue's hand reads: "There is no darkness but ignorance." Just opposite is a **statue of Charlie Chaplin;** thus, the square is consecrated to theater and cinema.

Walk along the path that leads away from Shakespeare. At the end of the path, you'll come to **Reynolds Gate,** named for Sir Joshua Reynolds, the celebrated 18th-century portrait painter and first president of the Royal Academy of Arts. Reynolds lived and painted at 47 Leicester Fields.

Walk counterclockwise around the square to **Hunter's Gate,** named for scientist John Hunter. A contemporary of Reynolds, Hunter was a medical researcher who amassed a collection of more than 10,500 anatomical specimens, all of which were initially housed at his Leicester Square residence. Hunter, a surgeon and anatomist, has been called the "father of scientific surgery."

Continue counterclockwise around the square past the **Half-Price Ticket Booth,** where you can buy discounted theater tickets on the day of performance only. The booth opens at noon for matinees and from 2:30 to 6:30pm for evening performances. Payment must be made in cash (traveler's checks and credit cards aren't accepted), and there's a small service charge.

The last gate is **Newton's Gate,** named for scientist, mathematician, and philosopher Sir Isaac Newton (1642–1727).

Exit the gardens at Newton's Gate and walk a little way to arrive outside the Moon Under Water Pub, which stands on the site of:

3. **28 Leicester Square,** where John Singleton Copley, a leading portrait painter, lived with his family from 1776 to 1783. On December 5, 1782, while Copley was working on a portrait of Elkanah Watson, the two adjourned

in order to hurry over to the House of Lords to hear George III announce the end of the American War of Independence. On their return, Watson said that Copley, "with a bold hand, a master's touch, and I believe an American heart," painted the stars and stripes on the flag flying from a ship in the background of the portrait. Watson later observed: "This, I imagine, was the first American flag hoisted in England."

When you reach Hogarth Gate (where you entered the gardens), turn left, continue counterclockwise around the square, and take the first right into Leicester Place; this was laid out and constructed in the 1790s by banker Thomas Wright. Half a block ahead on your right is:

4. **Notre Dame de France,** 5 Leicester Place, a skylight-topped round church founded by a Marist priest in 1865. The facade features a statue of Mater Misericordia while the carved pillars and reliefs portray eight scenes from the life of the Virgin Mary, all created by students from Paris's Ecole des Beaux-Arts. Inside, you'll find an unassuming altar made of Portland stone. The murals in the Blessed Sacrament Chapel, to your left, were painted in 1960 by Jean Cocteau, depicting the annunciation, Mary at the foot of the cross, and the assumption.

Exit the church, continue to the end of Leicester Place, and turn right onto:

5. **Lisle Street,** one of half a dozen streets just north of Leicester Square that comprise London's Chinatown. A stroll here will reveal block after block of Chinese restaurants, grocers, and herbalists. Once concentrated in the Docklands area, east of the City, London's Chinese community—then numbering some 2,000—began to migrate westward in the 1950s, seeking out new business opportunities. Chinese restaurants first opened in Soho after World War II to cater to British servicemen who had acquired a taste for this food overseas. At the time, Soho was dominated by shabby brothels, seedy nightclubs, and run-down restaurants. Since short-term leases could be obtained for rather modest sums, Chinese entrepreneurs began renting properties in this area, and so Chinatown was born. Today, there are many inexpensive but good Chinese restaurants here, most specializing in traditional Cantonese cuisine.

Continue right along Lisle Street; at the corner of Newport Place is the:

6. **Polar Bear Pub,** 30 Lisle St. (☎ **0171/437-3048**). Formerly called the White Bear, this tavern hosted some of the Rolling Stones' earliest rehearsals in 1962; their appearance was arranged by Brian Jones.

Turn left onto Newport Place, then turn left again under the Chinatown arch onto Gerrard Street—the bustling, colorful center of London's Chinatown. A few doors down, on your left, is:

7. **Loon Fung Supermarket,** 42–44 Gerrard St., a large Chinese market selling exotic food. Poet John Dryden (1631–1700) once lived unhappily with his wife in a house on this site. His wife once said that she'd like to be a book so that he'd pay more attention to her. Dryden replied, "Pray my dear . . . let it be an almanac, for then I shall change you every year." Reflecting further on his marriage, Dryden penned the following premature epitaph:

> *Here lies my wife, so let her lie*
> *Now she's at rest and so am I.*

Continue to the end of Gerrard Street, passing the two carved stone **Chinese lions** on your left (a donation from the People's Republic of China in 1985). Just beyond (also on the left) notice the two Chinese-style pagoda **telephone boxes.**

At the intersection of Wardour Street, turn right, cross Shaftesbury Avenue, and continue straight to the iron gates (on the right) that guard:

8. **St. Anne's Church Tower.** An entire church once stood here. Dedicated to Queen Anne by her tutor, Henry Compton, the chapel was built by Sir Christopher Wren in 1678 and destroyed by World War II bombs. Today, all that remains is this peculiar beer-barrel–shaped church tower, designed by architect Samuel Pepys Cockerell.

Walk through the gates and stand by the tower. Above the large tombstone on the wall to your right is a **tablet** commemorating Theodore, king of Corsica, "who died in this parish December 11, 1756." Forced from his kingdom, Theodore sought asylum in London but was soon imprisoned here for debt. Writer Horace Walpole composed the following epitaph for the king:

> *The grave, great teacher to a level brings*
> *heroes and beggars, galley slaves and kings*
> *but Theodore this moral learn ere dead*
> *fate poured its lessons on his living head*
> *bestowed a Kingdom and denied him bread.*

Exit the churchyard through the gates you entered, right on Wardour Street, and turn right again onto:

9. **Old Compton Street,** Soho's main shopping thorough-fare. It was named for Henry Compton, former Bishop of London. Old Compton today is very popular with London's gay community, and lining it are numerous cafes where patrons can dine alfresco as Soho's colorful street life drifts by.

Cross Old Compton Street, turn right, and then take the first left onto Dean Street. Continue to the corner of:

10. **Meard Street,** a short street that was a private project of carpenter John Meard—on the rowhouse wall, you can still see a plaque inscribed "Meards Street 1732."

Continue a short distance along Dean Street and stop outside:

11. **Leoni's Quo Vadis,** 26–29 Dean St. (☎ 0171/437-4809), a restaurant established by P. G. Leoni in 1926. Before it was a restaurant, however, this building was the home of Karl Marx; he and his family lived in two small upstairs rooms from 1851 to 1856. They subsisted on a small weekly sum given to them by their friend Friedrich Engels. Marx claimed that he rarely went out "because my clothes are in pawn." Three of his young children died here.

Backtrack along Dean Street and take the first left into Bateman Street. At the intersection with Frith Street on the left you'll find the:

☕ **Take a Break** **Dog and Duck Public House,** 18 Bateman St. (☎ 0171/437-4447), which has stood at this site since 1734. This is the quintessential "locals' pub" in Soho; its name recalls the rather cruel sport of duck hunting, which had been popular when the area was more rural. George Orwell chose this pub in which to celebrate the selection of *Animal Farm* by the American Book-of-the-Month Club.

Exit the pub right onto:

12. **Frith Street.** Initially named for its builder, Richard Frith, this commercial street was eventually called Thrift Street; around the turn of the century its original name was restored.

Continue along Frith Street for a half block, where, on your left, you'll see the stage entrance of the Prince Edward Theatre. This building stands on the site of the:

13. **Wolfgang Amadeus Mozart House,** 20 Frith St. Mozart (1756–91) was already a renowned prodigy (age 8) when his family came here to stay for 6 months. A local celebrity, Mozart attracted attention whenever he and his sister took walks around the neighborhood. The young composer gave a recital of his own works in this house, performing on a miniature violin that was specially made for him.

Retrace your steps along Frith Street for 1 block until, on the right, you arrive at:

14. **Hazlitt's Hotel,** 6 Frith St. The building dates from 1718 and is named for essayist William Hazlitt (1778–1830), a Renaissance man who began as a painter but then turned to writing essays for popular critical magazines. Hazlitt died in this building, with these words: "Well, I've had a happy life."

Continue to the end of Frith Street (on your left you'll pass the London headquarters of Twentieth Century Fox), which opens onto:

15. **Soho Square,** an attractive quiet square that somehow seems out of place amid the theaters, clubs, and shops just a few steps away. Laid out during the reign of Charles II, the square became home to the duke of Monmouth, the king's illegitimate son. An army officer, Monmouth made "Soho" the secret password at the Battle of Sedgemoor in 1685, where he was defeated in his attempt to oust Charles's successor, James II. Many of his co-conspirators were executed in what became known as the Bloody Assizes; the

duke himself was tried and later beheaded at the Tower of London.

The small black-and-white **wooden structure** at the center of the square is a toolhouse dating from the 1870s. Also in the square's gardens is a **statue of Charles II,** dating from 1681.

Walking counterclockwise around the square, stop at the corner of Greek Street to see the:

16. **House of St. Barnabus,** 1 Greek St. (☎ 0171/ **437-1894**), believed to have been the inspiration for Dr. Manette's house in Charles Dickens's *A Tale of Two Cities.* The house, from the mid-18th century, is noted for its extraordinarily detailed interior, complete with carved wood, rococo plasterwork, and wrought-iron staircase. Now serving as a temporary shelter for homeless women, the house is open to the public on Wednesday from 2:30 to 4:30pm and Thursday from 11am to 12:30pm.

Continue your counterclockwise circumambulation of the square. As you reach Soho Street you'll come to:

17. **10 Soho Square,** a late-17th-century building that was once the home of Lady Mary Wortley Montague, a gifted intellectual and writer. She was a leader of society and fashion and the friend (or enemy) of most of the literary figures of her time. Her contemporary, Horace Walpole, once described her as "old, foul, tawdry, painted, plastered. . . . She wears a foul mop that does not cover her greasy black locks that hang loose, never combed, never curled." Lady Mary might have married poet Alexander Pope, except that when he proposed, she laughed so long and loud that he immediately became one of her enemies.

The redbrick building on the opposite corner is the:

18. **French Protestant Church,** erected in the 16th century "in grateful memory of H. M. King Edward VI who, by his charter of 1550, granted asylum to the Huguenots from France."

Continue on to:

19. **2 Soho Square,** home of MPL Industries—the former Beatle Paul McCartney's London office.

Exit Soho Square by turning right onto Carlisle Street. Three hundred years ago here stood the:

20. **Home of the earl of Carlisle,** a gentleman who befriended an eccentric inventor named Joseph Merlin. In the 1760s, Merlin was working on what became his most notable invention—roller skates. One evening, during an elegant ball, the unorthodox Merlin demonstrated his skates by rolling at high speed through the mansion's salon, while playing the violin. Losing his balance, he crashed through an ornate—and very expensive—mirror, thus ending the demonstration and the ball.

Continue along Carlisle Street for 1 block, turn left onto Dean Street, and then turn right onto pedestrian St. Anne's Court. One block down, on your right, at:

21. **17 St. Anne's Court,** is a gray building that once housed the studio where the Beatles recorded several tracks of *The White Album* and "Hey Jude." The studio's grand piano was auctioned in 1989 for £30,000.

From St. Anne's Court, cross Wardour Street (home of many of London's most important film companies) and walk straight onto Broadwick Street. Just ahead, at the corner of Poland Street, is the:

22. **Broadwick Street Pump,** a water pump that was identified by Dr. John Snow as the source of the Soho cholera epidemic in 1854. Snow, a noted anesthetist who had studied cholera during a previous epidemic, theorized that polluted drinking water caused the disease. He plotted on a map the addresses of more than 500 people who died in September 1854 and discovered that the Broad Street Public Water Pump (as it was then called) was at the geographic center of the epidemic. Snow's theory initially met with disbelief, but when the doctor had the handle of the pump removed, preventing it from being used, the outbreak soon ended.

Continue 2 blocks to the end of Broadwick Street, past an elegant row of 18th-century houses, and turn left onto:

23. **Carnaby Street,** London's "fashion" center in the 1960s. This pedestrian-only thoroughfare was laid out in the 1680s and named for Karnaby House, an apartment complex for

a large number of Huguenot immigrants. The area slowly changed, and by the mid-19th century, the street was the home of tradespeople who owned neighborhood shops. In 1957, retailers John Stephens, John Vince, and Andreas Spyropoulus opened Carnaby Street's first boutique—a men's store that soon attracted other fashionable-clothing shops. In the 1960s, Carnaby Street became synonymous with "flower power." *Time* magazine focused international attention on this street, and the *Oxford English Dictionary* defined Carnaby Street as "fashionable clothing for young people."

Today, the world of high fashion has moved elsewhere, but Carnaby Street still has a number of clothing shops that are worth looking at.

At the end of Carnaby Street, turn left into Beak Street and walk about 2 blocks. On the left you'll come to:

24. **41 Beak St.,** home of Italian painter Antonio Canaletto (1697–1768) from 1749 to 1751. While living here, he advertised that he had a painting of his for sale, *A View of St. James's Park,* that would "be shown to any gentleman that will be pleased to come to his house."

Backtrack along Beak Street until you reach Upper John Street. Turn left and proceed to Golden Square, in the middle of which is a **statue of George II** (1683–1760) by an unknown sculptor. Walk around Golden Square until you come to:

25. **14 Golden Square,** where Thomas Jefferson leased rooms on March 11, 1786. John Adams had urged Jefferson to come to London from Paris. The two statesmen had hoped to take advantage of the presence in London of the ambassador of Tripolitania in order to resolve the issue of American ships being seized by Barbary Coast pirates. After a month of attending to diplomatic and social functions, Jefferson left for home with some relief. As he said to a friend: "This nation hates us, their ministers hate us, and their king more than any other man."

In order to visualize more accurately what Golden Square looked like in Jefferson's day, look at **nos. 23 and 24** (the Portuguese Embassy).

As you proceed into Lower John Street, notice the narrow building that's second along on the left:

26. **4 Lower John St.** This building, which was erected about 1685, was designed to have just one room on each floor.

Turn left into Brewer Street and walk about 2 blocks to:

27. **71 Brewer St.,** the former address of Chevalier De'eon. In 1762, De'eon arrived from France as an undercover agent for Louis XV, who was planning to invade England. The invasion never materialized, but the chevalier remained, befriending important Londoners and acquiring a reputation as one of the 18th century's most outrageous eccentrics. Part of his fascination arose from the fact that it wasn't clear whether the chevalier was a man or a woman. His features were beautiful and his figure curvaceous, but De'eon drank heavily, smoked cigars, and was an accomplished equestrian and duelist. The chevalier deliberately encouraged speculation by openly denying that he was a man, even though he dressed as one. In gentlemen's clubs, bets were placed on his sex (seven to four that he was a man). Many of those bets were collected several years later, when the chevalier began appearing in public dressed as a woman. By the time he died in 1816, at age 82, London accepted De'eon as a woman. When a postmortem exam revealed that he was indeed a man, the disclosure took the city by surprise.

Continue walking along Brewer Street, which (from this point) epitomizes the essence of Soho. The street is lined with an incredible variety of shops—from peep shows and hostess bars to traditional village shops.

Somewhat farther along Brewer Street you'll arrive on the left at:

Winding Down **Randall and Aubin,** 16 Brewer St. (☎ **0171/437-3507** or 0171/437-3508). Specializing in charcuterie and patisserie, this "high-class deli" has changed little since it opened in 1911. It specializes in home-cooked cold meats and substantial sandwiches.

Continue walking along Brewer Street; take the first right turn into Rupert Street and proceed 2 blocks to Shaftesbury Avenue. Turn right and continue ahead to Piccadilly Circus Underground Station.

Chelsea

Start: Sloane Square Underground Station.

Finish: Sloane Square Underground Station.

Time: 2 hours.

Best Times: Wednesday to Saturday from 10am to noon and 2 to 4pm, when all the interiors included in this tour are open; Saturday on King's Road is particularly lively.

Worst Times: At night and on Sunday (when most shops on King's Road are closed).

$\quad$ Chelsea is an incredibly expensive residential area, but that wasn't always the case. Stretching along the Thames, south of Hyde Park and Kensington, Chelsea gained fame in the 19th century as London's Bohemia, a place for writers, artists, musicians, and thinkers. This beautiful "town within a city" was home to Thomas Carlyle, George Eliot, J. M. W. Turner, John Singer Sargent, Oscar Wilde, Henry James—the list of famous former residents seems endless.

$\quad$ But times change, and in the 20th century Chelsea was discovered by a new group of Londoners. Its location and beauty have turned it into a favorite stomping ground of the monied classes. This tour will take you through one of the world's most beautiful urban neighborhoods. Take a close look at Chelsea—you've probably never seen so many appealing homes that you'd like to own.

• • • • • • • • • • • • • • • •

Exit Sloane Square Underground Station, turn right, and walk a few steps to the:

1. **Royal Court Theatre,** Sloane Square (☎ 0171/ 730-1745). Opened in 1888, the Royal Court quickly gained a top reputation by staging George Bernard Shaw's plays; many of them were rehearsed and performed here under his personal direction. After serving as a cinema in the 1930s and suffering bomb damage during World War II, the theater was rebuilt and became home to the English Stage Company—one of the city's most innovative theatrical groups. With the premiere of John Osborne's *Look Back in Anger* in 1956, the Royal Court has attracted many leading dramatists to make their debuts at this theater, which is known for consistently high-quality productions.

Buy a ticket for the evening's performance, then retrace your steps past Sloane Square Station and continue straight ahead to:

2. **Sloane Gardens,** named for Sir Hans Sloane (1660–1753), who served as president of the Royal Society for 14 years. Sloane, who lived nearby, gained fame for his collection of more than 800 plant and animal specimens, which he kept in his home. Upon his death, Sloane bequeathed 50,000 books and thousands of manuscripts to the British Museum—a windfall for their emerging collection.

The magnificent redbrick houses lining both sides of Sloane Gardens were built by developer/parliamentarian William Willett, who, incidentally, was the chief campaigner for the establishment of Summer Time (daylight saving time) in 1889.

Located just after the bend in the street is:

3. **49 Sloane Gardens,** the former home of novelist/ dramatist Egerton Castle (1858–1926), who lived here during the last years of his life.

At the end of Sloane Gardens, turn left onto the busier Lower Sloane Street. Continue 2 blocks past the upscale shops, down to the traffic lights, and cross the road to the:

4. **Old Burial Ground,** the cemetery of the adjacent Chelsea Royal Hospital (see Stop 6). Peek through the iron railings. A soldier, Simon Box, was the first to be buried here, in 1692. Two of the more unusual stones are those of Robert Cumming and Joshua Cueman, which claim that on their deaths—in the 18th century—the men were aged 116 and 123, respectively. William Hiseland's 1732 headstone says that he was in the army for 80 years and "when a hundred years old he took unto him a wife." It would appear that the Chelsea Royal Hospital had been extremely successful in preserving the lives of its patients. Two women are interred here; both Christian David and Hanah Bell followed their lovers into battle in the Crimean War, each disguising herself as a male soldier. Their secrets weren't discovered until they were wounded in action. For lack of additional burial space, the Old Burial Ground had to close in 1854.

Though there are few tombstones, the cemetery is believed to be the final resting place of more than 10,000 former soldiers. Alas, the cemetery isn't open to the public, but you can see almost everything through the surrounding fence.

Turn right onto Royal Hospital Road with the cemetery to your left. After 100 yards, turn left and walk through two sets of gates called London Gate and Garden Gate, respectively. On your left is:

5. **Ranelagh Gardens,** one of 18th-century London's favorite outdoor areas. Enter the gardens. From 1742 to 1805, Ranelagh was the site of the Great Rotunda, an amusement park and meeting place for the upper classes. Eighteenth-century politician and man of letters Horace Walpole wrote, "Every night constantly I go to Ranelagh . . . my Lord Chesterfield is so fond of it that he says he has ordered all his letters to be directed thither." Today the Royal Hospital, which looms over the gardens, is the only remaining building in this park. With their gentle slope toward the Thames, the wooded and flowered greens of Ranelagh are some of the prettiest in London and a pleasure to stroll. The gates you entered are this park's only entrance; they close daily from 1 to 2pm.

Leave the gardens and turn right. Retrace your steps through Garden Gate, turn left into the driveway, and walk

Chelsea

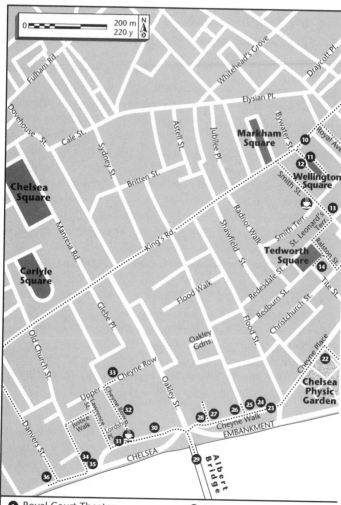

1. Royal Court Theater
2. Sloane Gardens
3. 49 Sloane Gardens
4. Old Burial Ground
5. Ranelagh Gardens
6. Chelsea Royal Hospital
7. Duke of York's Headquarters
8. Royal Avenue
9. 18 St. Leonard's Terrace
10. King's Road
11. Wellington Square
12. 32 Wellington Square
13. Victorian-era mailbox
14. 23 Tedworth Square
15. Durham Cottage
16. 34 Tite St.
17. 31 Tite St.
18. 33 Tite St.
19. Whitehouse
20. Paradise Walk
21. Clover Mews
22. Chelsea Physic Garden
23. Cheyne Walk
24. 2 Cheyne Walk

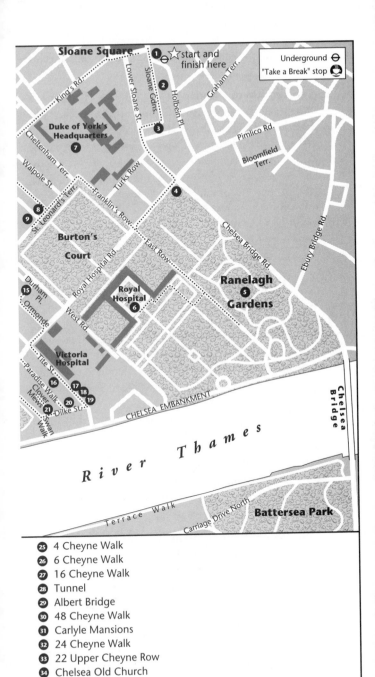

straight through the wooden doors into the central court of the:

6. **Chelsea Royal Hospital.** Designed by Sir Christopher Wren (architect of St. Paul's Cathedral), the hospital was founded in 1682 by Charles II for men "broken by war and old age." Inspired by the Hôtel des Invalides in Paris, the Chelsea Royal Hospital still serves as a home for elderly, unmarried war veterans with no other source of income. Today, there are about 420 "Chelsea pensioners." Male veterans over 65 receive food, shelter, and clothing plus a small weekly allowance, which they happily supplement by showing visitors around the buildings. You can easily identify the pensioners by their scarlet or blue uniforms and tricornered hats, which they wear on special occasions.

Walk past the **statue of Charles II** and enter the hospital through the main door, under the clock. On your right is the **chapel,** featuring a relatively bright interior that's typical of Wren churches. On your left is the **Great Hall,** an awe-inspiring wood-paneled dining room that would probably transform even the most mundane meal into an exquisite banquet. The painting on the left wall is of Charles II on horseback.

The Chelsea Royal Hospital is open to the public Monday to Saturday from 10am to noon and 2 to 4pm and Sunday from 2 to 4pm.

Return to Royal Hospital Road, cross the pedestrian walkway, and continue straight ahead on Franklin's Row. With the private cricket grounds and tennis courts on your left, walk 1 block to the:

7. **Duke of York's Headquarters,** the large compound on your right, surrounded by an iron railing. Now used as a barracks for the Territorial Army—England's National Guard—the complex was built in 1801 as a school for war-orphaned children. The duke for whom this property was named was the second son of George III and head of the English army. The Duke of York earned a reputation as a military reformer because he tried to stop the widespread buying and selling of army commissions. The number of officers who were unfit for their position had grown so large that the duke had to ask for the resignations of all colonels under age 20 and all captains under age 12! Ironically, it

was later discovered that the duke's mistress was one of the people who were selling commissions, and he was forced to resign in disgrace. The Duke of York's Headquarters isn't open to the public.

Turn left onto St. Leonard's Terrace and walk 1 block to arrive at:

8. **Royal Avenue,** a romantically quiet and picturesque street lined with tall redbrick houses from the early 19th century. The street was laid out in 1682 by Sir Christopher Wren; he intended it to be part of a direct route from the Chelsea Royal Hospital to Kensington Palace. However, this short block was the only part of the project that had been completed by 1685, when Charles II, the plan's sponsor, died. The rest of the route was never finished.

Continue along St. Leonard's Terrace to the row of houses on the right, where a blue plaque at:

9. **18 St. Leonard's Terrace** commemorates the former home of Bram Stoker (1847–1912). A prolific author, Stoker moved here in 1896, the year before his most famous book, *Dracula,* was published.

Retrace your footsteps to turn left into Royal Avenue. Continue to its end and turn left onto:

10. **King's Road,** Chelsea's primary commercial thoroughfare. Laid out in the 17th century, this originally was the king's road, a private street built exclusively for Charles II, enabling him to travel from his London home to Hampton Court Palace. The only people allowed to use this road were the king and holders of a special copper pass with a crown on one side and the words "The King's Private Road" on the other. King's Road remained private until the 1830s. Now celebrated for its shops and boutiques, this is one of London's best shopping streets. It's especially crowded on Saturday, when some of the city's trendiest young people transform it into an informal fashion show.

Walk 1 block and turn left into:

11. **Wellington Square,** a delightfully picturesque horseshoe named for the duke of Wellington. Built around 1830, the square has been home to several famous residents, including A. A. Milne (1882–1956), creator of Winnie the Pooh, who lived at no. 8 from 1904 to 1906, in what he later

described as "two cheap and dirty rooms" at the top of the house. (Milne also lived nearby, on Mallord Street, for almost 30 years.) While living on Wellington Square, Milne wrote his first book, *Lovers in London*.

Walk around the square to **no. 30.** This was the presumed home of fictional hero James Bond, though not specifically pinpointed by his creator, Ian Fleming. Close by you'll see:

12. **32 Wellington Square,** where American novelist Thomas Wolfe (1900–38) lived for a year, during which he wrote *Look Homeward, Angel,* one of his best-known works.

Back on King's Road, turn left, walk 1 block, and turn left onto Smith Street. On the next corner is the:

☕ **Take a Break** **Resident,** 23 Smith St. (☎ 0171/730-7721), where you can avoid the tourists from King's Road and take a tipple with the locals. There are always special rotating "guest" beers, as well as the most popular brands. Food choices include sausages, sandwiches, pasta, vegetarian dishes, and hot meat pies.

Continue 1 block down Smith Street where, at the corner of St. Leonard's Terrace, you'll see a:

13. **Victorian-era mailbox.** Shaped like a pillar, the thickly painted red box incorporates the Royal Badge (a lion and a unicorn) and the initials "VR" (for Victoria Regina) above an extremely narrow mail slot.

Turn right onto St. Leonard's Terrace and proceed to Tedworth Square. Walk clockwise around the square to:

14. **23 Tedworth Square,** the former home of Mark Twain (Samuel Langhorne Clemens, 1835–1910). Twain gained fame and fortune writing American classics like *The Adventures of Tom Sawyer* (1873) and *The Adventures of Huckleberry Finn* (1885). However, he lived extravagantly and invested poorly; thus, in 1891, the bankrupt Twain fled to Europe to escape his creditors. After his daughter, Susy, died in August 1896, Twain secluded himself in this house. The following year, the *New York Herald* newspaper set up a fund to collect money to repay Twain's debts, enabling his return to America.

Backtrack to the corner and cross toward no. 13, turn right into Ralston Street, and at the end of that street turn left into Christchurch Street. One block along on the left, pause outside the light-blue gate of:

15. **Durham Cottage,** 4 Christchurch St., the former home of Sir Laurence Olivier and Vivien Leigh, who scandalized "polite" society by becoming involved while they were both still married to others. They moved here in May 1937, and Vivien set about decorating and furnishing the house in Regency style, complete with antiques and artworks. One observer thought that the house had an "almost claustrophobic prettiness" where Olivier was like "an unfortunate bull in a china shop."

On November 5, 1938, they invited Ralph Richardson and his wife here to celebrate Vivien's birthday. Since it was also Guy Fawkes night, Richardson arrived with a box of fireworks and went into the garden to set off a rocket. Alas, the firecracker flew straight back into the dining room, burning the new curtains, of which Vivien was extremely proud, and destroying antique crockery. Vivien was furious. Richardson summoned his wife and attempted to leave, but as he reached the door, the handle came off in his hand.

Retrace your footsteps along Christchurch Street and make the first left into Ormonde Gate. Turn right at the end into Royal Hospital Road, then make the first left into Tite Street. A little way along, on the right, is:

16. **34 Tite St.,** the former home of Oscar Wilde (1854–1900). When the controversial Irish wit and dramatist moved here in 1885, he was already a celebrity. The author of such works as *The Importance of Being Earnest* and *The Picture of Dorian Gray,* Wilde lived here for 10 years. It was here, in 1891, that Wilde was introduced to his lover, Lord Alfred Douglas (known as Bosie), son of the marquess of Queensberry. Douglas's father disapproved of their relationship, even going so far as to once turn up here carrying a horse whip, intent on thrashing Wilde.

Another time, an attempt was made to blackmail Wilde, when a man named Allen arrived with a letter Wilde had written to Bosie. When the would-be extortionist remarked,

"A very curious construction can be put on this letter," Wilde replied that "art is rarely intelligible to the criminal classes." Allen pointed out that "a man has offered me £60 for it." Wilde told him to "go to that man and sell my letter to him. I myself have never received so large a sum for any prose work of that length; but I am glad to find that there is someone in England who considers a letter of mine worth £60."

Meanwhile, the marquess of Queensberry continued his vendetta. When he left a note at Wilde's club, the Albermarle, addressed to "Oscar Wilde posing as a Somdomite [sic]," the author brought suit against the marquess for libel. Wilde lost and became subject to prosecution as a homosexual, a criminal offense in England until 1967. The authorities gave him time to leave the country, but the defiant Wilde chose instead to sip champagne at the nearby Cadogan Hotel, where he was arrested. Upon conviction, Wilde was sentenced to 2 years of hard labor. After being released, he went into exile in Paris, where he died in poverty in 1900.

Continue half a block farther down Tite Street to:

17. **31 Tite St.,** the former home of John Singer Sargent (1856–1925). The American artist lived and worked in this house until his death on April 15, 1925.

Two doors down is:

18. **33 Tite St.,** the former studio of Augustus John (1879–1961). One of the best-loved Welsh portraitists, John was a founding member of the De Stijl movement. He epitomized the English bohemian of the 1950s. The bearded, charismatic painter defied social convention in his dress, behavior, and way of life. An infamous womanizer, John attracted and mistreated numerous women.

Look at the light-brown brick building (with the lantern over the black door) next door on your left. This was once the site of the:

19. **Whitehouse,** a grand home built in the 1870s for American painter James Abbott McNeill Whistler (1834–1903). While the house was still under construction, Whistler brought a slander suit against art critic John Ruskin because of his review of Whistler's painting *Nocturne in*

Black and Gold: The Falling Rocket. Ruskin wrote: "I never expected to hear a coxcomb ask 200 guineas for flinging a pot of paint in the public's face." Though Whistler won the case, he was awarded only one farthing (a quarter-cent) in damages and was ordered to pay his own enormous legal costs. Temporarily bankrupt, the painter was forced to sell his beloved Whitehouse.

Turn right onto Dilke Street and right again onto:

20. **Paradise Walk,** a tranquil block lined with a pretty row of cottages trimmed with shuttered windows. The street wasn't always this bucolic, however; in fact, in the late 19th century, it was such a slum that Oscar Wilde erected a screen in his backyard so that he wouldn't have to look at it.

Return to Dilke Street and take the next right onto:

21. **Clover Mews,** another pretty street that helps to make Chelsea one of the most desirable neighborhoods in London. The word *mews* comes from the French word *muer* ("to molt"). Originally a place where hawks were kept while molting, mews evolved to become buildings with stables on the ground floor and living quarters upstairs. Eventually mews referred to the small streets where such buildings were located.

Return to Dilke Street and take the next right onto Swan Walk. Look through the iron gate on your left at the:

22. **Chelsea Physic Garden** (☎ 0171/352-5646), the second oldest physic garden in England (the one in Oxford is older). Originally established by the Apothecaries' Company in 1673 for cultivating medicinal plants, the garden has since expanded to include rare species from the New World. Behind its high walls is a rare collection of exotic plants, shrubs, and trees—many of them more than 100 years old. An unusual rock garden features stone from the Tower of London and basaltic lava from Iceland. Cotton seeds were sent from this garden to Georgia colonist James Oglethorpe in 1732, which helped to establish the cotton industry of the American South.

The garden is open April to October only, Wednesday from 2 to 5pm and Sunday from 2 to 6pm. The resident English Gardening School holds lectures throughout the summer. Call for details.

Turn left around the gardens to Cheyne Place; after 2 blocks, bear right (across Flood Street) onto:

23. **Cheyne Walk,** one of the most celebrated streets in Chelsea. The houses on Cheyne (rhymes with "rainy") were built in 1720 and have been owned by famous people in the arts and entertainment field for more than a century.

    A few steps ahead is:

24. **2 Cheyne Walk,** the house that John Barrymore leased in November 1924. He'd just finished performing *Hamlet* in New York and decided that he wanted to try the role before London audiences. Since he couldn't find an English producer willing to take a chance on an American actor in this role, Barrymore financed the production himself. He leased the Haymarket Theatre and the play opened on February 19, 1925. In the audience on opening night were such luminaries as John Masefield, Somerset Maugham, Arnold Bennett, and George Bernard Shaw. The drama critic of the *Sunday Times* praised Barrymore's performance: "We know ourselves to be in the presence of a fine and powerful mind."

    Just beyond, you'll come to:

25. **4 Cheyne Walk,** the former home of novelist George Eliot (Mary Ann Evans, 1819–80). Throughout much of her life, Eliot was enveloped in scandal for living with a married man, literary critic George Henry Lewes. Often treated as a social pariah, Eliot found it extremely uncomfortable to appear in public with her lover. After Lewes died in 1878, Eliot became involved with John Cross, whom she later married. The couple moved to this house in 1880, but their time together was short, since Eliot died just a few months later—in December 1880. On his wife's death, Cross wrote in his diary, " . . . and I am left alone in this new house we were meant to be so happy in."

    Two doors down, at:

26. **6 Cheyne Walk,** you can see an excellently preserved example of the block's original 1720s architecture. Notice the two metal plaques above and to the left of the front door. These are insurance markers, indicating that the house was insured by two fire companies. Unlike modern-day practice, late-18th-century policies didn't promise to repay

damages. To have insurance meant that if your house caught fire, the company you paid would come to put it out; there were no public fire departments. The top plaque shows the clasped hands of the Amicable Contributors Company. The lower plaque, depicting a lion in a circle, was issued by the British Fire Office.

One block ahead is:

27. **16 Cheyne Walk,** the former home of Dante Gabriel Rossetti (1828–82). The 19th-century painter/poet lived and worked in this handsome Tudor house from 1862 until his death. A member of the Pre-Raphaelite group, he moved here soon after the death of his wife, Elizabeth Siddal. When she was buried, the distraught Rossetti had a volume of his love poetry wrapped in her long hair and entombed with her. Seven years later, however, he had second thoughts about his romantic gesture, exhumed his manuscript, and published the poems.

Quite the eccentric, Rossetti turned his home into a sort of menagerie, filling it with a collection of exotic animals. In addition to a kangaroo and a raccoon, the artist kept a white bull, whose antics turned the garden into a wasteland. He also had a wombat that was much admired by his friend Lewis Carroll; it inspired Carroll to create the dormouse for *Alice in Wonderland.*

About 50 yards ahead on Cheyne Walk, turn right into the:

28. **Tunnel** that runs between nos. 23 and 24 Cheyne Walk. Henry VIII's country house stood here until 1753, when it was demolished following the death of its last occupant, Sir Hans Sloane (see Stop 2). The cautionary sign at the entrance to the tunnel on your left reads: "All drivers of vehicles are directed to *walk* their horses while passing under this archway."

Return to Cheyne Walk and continue to the corner of Oakley Street. On your left you'll see:

29. **Albert Bridge,** one of the most picturesque spans in the world. Constructed at the height of the Victorian fascination with cast iron, it was designed in 1873 by R. M. Ordish.

Cross Oakley Street and continue along Cheyne Walk. One block ahead on your right is:

30. **48 Cheyne Walk,** the former home of the Rolling Stones' lead singer, Mick Jagger, who lived here in the early 1970s. Band member Charley Watts still lives nearby.

    At the corner of Cheyne Row and Cheyne Walk is the:

    ☕ **Take a Break** **Kings Head and Eight Bells,** 50 Cheyne Walk (☎ **0171/352-1820**). Opened around 1580, this intimate pub has long been a favorite of local writers and artists. The high concentration of luminaries who live in this area has always meant star clientele. The tavern's clublike atmosphere mirrors the exclusiveness of the neighborhood. In addition to a full line of ales and bitters, the pub boasts great food.

    Exit the pub and continue along Cheyne Walk. The building next door is:

31. **Carlyle Mansions,** where the newly married Ian Fleming leased a third-floor riverview apartment in 1952. Fleming jested that he'd started writing novels in order to overcome the shock of getting married at the age of 44. Although he began work on *Casino Royale* while on the island of Jamaica, he revised it in his apartment here. He derived his hero's name, James Bond, from the name of an ornithologist whose volume on birds sat on his breakfast table.

    Backtrack along Cheyne Walk and turn left into Cheyne Row; walk half a block to:

32. **24 Cheyne Row** (☎ **0171/352-7087**), the beautifully preserved former residence of Thomas Carlyle (1795–1881), one of Britain's most important essayists and historians. Carlyle lived here a long time—from 1834 until his death. The house, dating from 1702, is now a museum administered by the National Trust. It's maintained much as it was in Carlyle's day, when the address was 5 Cheyne Row (notice that the "5" has been crossed out). There are still no electric lights on the upper floors.

    While living here, Carlyle completed his epic *History of the French Revolution.* He lent the only manuscript of the first volume to John Stuart Mill, who, shortly thereafter, hurried to Carlyle's door to confess that his maid had "taken it for waste paper" and burned it. Carlyle had to rewrite the entire volume from memory, confessing at the end that he felt like a man who had "nearly killed himself accomplishing zero." A visit to this house is a *must*. It's open April to the end of October, Wednesday to Sunday and bank holiday Mondays from 11am to 5pm. There's an admission charge.

Walk half a block to the end of Cheyne Row and turn right onto Upper Cheyne Row; a few yards down on your left is:

33. **22 Upper Cheyne Row,** the former home of Leigh Hunt (1784–1859), an essayist/poet who lived here from 1833 to 1840. A contemporary and friend of poets Byron, Keats, and Shelley, Hunt loved Chelsea and once wrote about this neighborhood:

"The end of the world. The air of the neighboring river so refreshing and the quiet of the 'no thoroughfare' so full of repose that although our fortunes were at their worst, and my health almost of a piece with them, I felt for some weeks as if I could sit still for ever, embalmed in silence."

Retrace your steps to the corner of Cheyne Row and continue straight ahead, where the road curves left into Lawrence Street. Walk 1 block down Lawrence Street, turn right onto the narrow Justice Walk, then turn left onto Old Church Street to the tall brick:

34. **Chelsea Old Church,** the parish church of Sir Thomas More (1478–1535). The building's beauty is diminished only by the heavy traffic outside and the fact that it and the surrounding area were heavily damaged by bombs during World War II. Gracefully repaired, the church has a chapel designed in part by Hans Holbein; an urn that contains the remains of a man who owned most of Chelsea during the 1700s, Sir Hans Sloane; and a plaque commemorating the life of American novelist Henry James, a longtime Chelsea resident who died nearby in 1916. The Lawrence Chapel is supposed to have been the scene of Henry VIII's secret marriage to Jane Seymour several days before their official marriage in 1536.

Outside the church, on the corner is a:

35. **Statue of Sir Thomas More,** good friend and chancellor of Henry VIII. When Henry broke with the Roman Catholic church, More refused to accept the king as head

of the Church of England—a stance for which he was subsequently beheaded on Tower Hill. More's story is depicted in the play and film *A Man for All Seasons.*

Cross Old Church Street; keeping the Thames to your left, walk down the steps and through the sunken garden. Walk up the steps at the other side of the garden, cross Danvers Street, and turn right into:

36. **Crosby Hall,** an ornate reception hall that was once part of the home of Sir John Crosby, a wealthy wool merchant. The Hall was built in the early 1400s and owned successively by both Richard III and Sir Thomas More. Its original, chapel-like brick-and-stone construction now has a modern wing of gray stone that was added in the 1950s. The Hall has no identifying street number, possibly because it was transported here stone by stone in the early 1900s from Bishopsgate in the City, under the partial sponsorship of American-born Lady Nancy Astor. Today the Hall is private property and not open to the public.

With your back to the river, walk up Danvers Street and turn right onto King's Road. From here you can either take a leisurely 1-mile stroll back to Sloane Square Underground Station, along the King's Road, stopping to admire its boutiques and shops. Or you can catch bus no. 11 or 22 for the return trip to Sloane Square.

Hampstead

Start: Hampstead Underground Station.

Finish: Hampstead Underground Station.

Time: 2 hours.

Best Times: Monday to Saturday between 2 and 5pm, when Keats's House is likely to be open.

Worst Times: Sunday, when shops on Hampstead High Street are closed.

London's most famous suburb, Hampstead gained fame as a 17th- and 18th-century spa resort. Situated on a ridge overlooking the City and the Thames, Hampstead is centered around a heath (785 acres of wild royal parkland) about 4 miles north of the center of London. In addition to high-rent homes and a bright shopping street, Hampstead's varied landscape includes formal park lands, woods, and ponds.

Hampstead's spas had fallen into disrepair by the mid-18th century, but the heath remained the traditional playground of the Londoner—the "'Appy 'Ampstead" of cockney legend—which had been dedicated "to the use of the public forever" by a special Act of Parliament in 1872.

"Leafy Hampstead," as it became known, has always attracted city dwellers eager to escape the grime and squalor of urban life. This suburb is most often associated with landscape painter John Constable and poet John Keats; regardless of famous residents and beautiful buildings, you'll enjoy strolling around one of England's loveliest pastures.

• • • • • • • • • • • • • • • •

Exit Hampstead Underground Station and turn left onto Heath Street. Continue straight about 2 blocks, until you reach a pedestrian crossing. Cross the road and you'll be at:

1. **Church Row,** often praised as one of the most attractive streets in Hampstead. Most of the carefully preserved houses on this block, dating from the 18th century, seem to be unspoiled by time. Walk down the left side of Church Row, noticing that an old lamp bracket remains on the corner, guarding the memory of its bygone gas lamp.

   A few doors down on your left is:

2. **26 Church Row,** the former home of Lord Alfred Douglas. He was the son of the marquess of Queensberry but was better known as Oscar Wilde's lover Bosie (for more information on Wilde, see Stop 16 in Walking Tour 10).

   Continue straight ahead, toward St. John's Church, and enter through the wrought-iron church gates known as the:

3. **Handel Gates.** They came from Cannon Park, Edgware, in 1747. It was there that George Frideric Handel served as composer for the duke of Chandos.

   Turn left immediately inside the church's gates and follow the rough, unpaved path that runs past the aged gravestones. Walk all the way to the bottom and turn right onto the paved path. Behind an iron fence to your left is:

4. **John and Maria Constable's grave.** John Constable (1776–1837), one of England's greatest landscape painters, moved to Hampstead in 1819 so that his family "might enjoy fresher air than London could provide." Indeed, Hampstead provided Constable with much more than fresh air; it inspired him to create some of his best works. Over the next 15 years, he painted Hampstead's heath, houses, trees, and clouds. By his own admission, Constable's happiest years were spent in Hampstead, of which he said, "Here, let me take my everlasting rest."

Hampstead

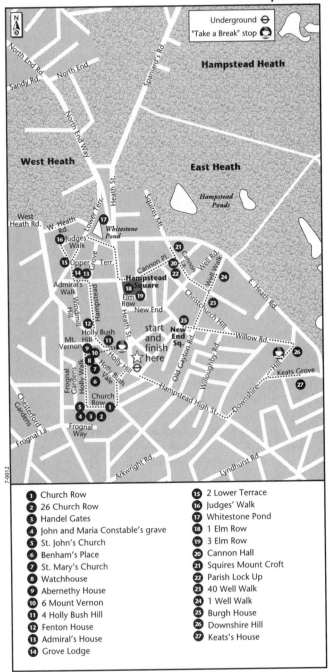

1. Church Row
2. 26 Church Row
3. Handel Gates
4. John and Maria Constable's grave
5. St. John's Church
6. Benham's Place
7. St. Mary's Church
8. Watchhouse
9. Abernethy House
10. 6 Mount Vernon
11. 4 Holly Bush Hill
12. Fenton House
13. Admiral's House
14. Grove Lodge
15. 2 Lower Terrace
16. Judges' Walk
17. Whitestone Pond
18. 1 Elm Row
19. 3 Elm Row
20. Cannon Hall
21. Squires Mount Croft
22. Parish Lock Up
23. 40 Well Walk
24. 1 Well Walk
25. Burgh House
26. Downshire Hill
27. Keats's House

With your back to the gravestone, walk on the path through the bushes to:

5. **St. John's Church.** The present building, from 1745, rests on medieval foundations. When the structure was enlarged in the 19th century, the entire church was reoriented, making it one of the few churches in the city with an altar that faces west rather than east (the direction of Jerusalem).

One hundred years ago, when the church's tower was facing possible demolition, it was saved only through the efforts of such local artists as Anthony Trollope, William Morris, and Holman Hunt.

Enter the church's octagonal vestibule, which used to be the vestry. To your right are **tablets** listing the church's vicars, past and present. Directly ahead, on your left, is a bronze **bas-relief of Henry Cort.** According to Charles H. Morgan, the eminent American engineer who commissioned it, the bronze work honors the man "to whom the world is indebted for the arts of refining iron by paddling with mineral coal and of rolling metals in grooved rolls." Once you enter through the church's inner doors, you'll see a charming gray-wood interior. Before you go down the central aisle, look to the left at the proud old **font** with the carved figure of John the Baptist on top. When facing the altar, you can see the church's old **pulpit** on your left. Above the radiator, to the right of the altar, is a **bust of poet John Keats,** presented "to the English Nation" in 1894 by a group of his American admirers. Because Keats spent much of his life in Hampstead and wrote some of his finest works here, it was decided to place the statue in this church, rather than in Westminster Abbey.

Climb the stairs to the right of Keats's bust. The small **cupboard** on your right was built to hold the loaves of bread that used to be given to the parish's poor. Turning left onto the balcony, you can stand in front of the church's **High Altar.**

Exit St. John's and walk down the pathway to your left. Go through the gates, cautiously cross the busy road, and walk straight ahead into Holly Walk. At the end of the graveyard, look to your right at:

6. **Benham's Place,** a quaint street lined with nine pretty cottages dating from 1813. These homes were built as part

of a development undertaken by William Benham, a grocer and cheese seller on Hampstead High Street.

A few yards down Holly Walk, on your right, is:

7. **St. Mary's Church,** a 1796 chapel built by and for refugees who fled their homeland during the French Revolution. St. Mary's was one of the first Roman Catholic churches to open in London after the Reformation. General Charles de Gaulle worshiped here during World War II.

A few steps ahead on your right is the:

8. **Watchhouse,** 9 Holly Place, the 1830s headquarters of Hampstead's first police force. Not everyone was pleased with the new constabulary, however. Many residents, including members of the local council, protested that police protection would place an undue burden on local taxpayers.

Step into Holly Berry Lane to savor its charm, then return to Holly Place and turn right. At the end of Holly Place, go right to Mount Vernon and stop outside the first house on your right. This is:

9. **Abernethy House,** a former girls' school that became a lodging house in the late 19th century. Robert Louis Stevenson (1850–94), who wrote *Treasure Island, Kidnapped,* and *Dr. Jekyll and Mr. Hyde,* stayed here several times. A booster of this charming suburb, Stevenson once remarked to a Scottish friend, "Hampstead is the most delightful place for air and scenery in London. I cannot understand how the air is so good, it does not explain itself to me."

Next door, at:

10. **6 Mount Vernon,** you can see a metal plaque above the front door. This is an insurance marker—proof that the house is covered by a fire company. Unlike modern insurance, late 18th-century policies didn't promise to repay any damage. Having insurance meant that if your house caught fire, the company you paid would come to put it out.

At the end of Mount Vernon on the left is a **blue plaque** marking the home of physiologist Sir Henry Dale. Walk along the pathway across from Dale's house, keeping left around the bend. Cross Holly Hill onto Holly Mount. A short way down on the left side is the:

Take a Break Holly Bush Pub, 22 Holly Mount, Heath Street (☎ 0171/435-2892). This tavern is closely associated with 18th-century painter George Romney, who purchased several properties nearby in 1796. When his health failed a few years later, Romney returned to his estranged wife in the Lake District; his stables were leased out and converted into this delightful tavern. It offers good food served in several charming gas lamp–lit rooms. Burton and Tetley bitters are always on tap.

Leave the pub, turn left, and walk to the end of Holly Mount, where you'll be rewarded with a spectacular, though obstructed, view over London.

Backtrack down Holly Mount. Turn right onto Holly Bush Hill and walk five doors up to:

11. **4 Holly Bush Hill,** the former home of George Romney (1734–1802). A relatively well-to-do artist who moved here in 1796, Romney had deserted his wife several years earlier, saying that "art and marriage do not mix." The artist's success as a portrait painter ended in 1797 (only a year after he had built this studio) owing to physical and mental illness. According to Romney's biographer, a friend noted in 1799 that his "increasing weakness of body and mind afforded only a gloomy prospect for the remainder of his life." Romney left Hampstead that year and returned to his wife in the Lake District, where he died a few years later.

The magnificent wrought-iron and gold-leaf gates across the street are the entrance to:

12. **Fenton House,** Windmill Hill (☎ 0171/435-3471), the oldest mansion in Hampstead, dating from 1693. Originally known as Ostend House, it was owned by silk merchant Joshua Gee, whose initials appear on the gates. Gee had close American connections and is known to have traded with George Washington's father. The merchant imported pig-iron from Maryland and became a landholder in Pennsylvania.

Bequeathed to the National Trust in 1952, Fenton House now houses the Binning collection of furniture and porcelain (most of it dating from the 18th century) as well as the Benton Fletcher collection of early keyboard instruments (some of which you may play).

The house is open in March on Saturday and Sunday from 2 to 6pm and April to October on Saturday to Wednesday from 11am to 6pm. There's an admission charge.

Continue uphill past the house's gates onto Hampstead Grove. Turn left onto Admiral's Walk and head to:

13. **Admiral's House.** Built around 1700, this house is notable for its roof, which, in 1791, was adapted to look like a ship's deck by Lt. Fountain North, who lived here from 1775 until his death in 1811. North even installed two cannons, which he'd fire to celebrate royal birthdays and naval victories. Sir George Gilbert Scott, the architect of Royal Albert Hall, lived here in the late 19th century.

Next door is:

14. **Grove Lodge,** the former home of John Galsworthy (1867–1933). Best known for his multivolume *Forsyte Saga,* Galsworthy won the 1932 Nobel Prize for literature. As he was too ill to receive his award in person, a delegation brought it to him here.

Continue along Admiral's Walk and turn right onto Lower Terrace. Bear right across the grass triangle and you'll arrive at:

15. **2 Lower Terrace,** a small house that was rented by artist John Constable during the summers of 1821 and 1822. Constable completed several oil paintings here, including one of Admiral's House and one of the shed in the back garden.

Facing the house, walk to the right along Lower Terrace, turn left, and cross over Upper Terrace to enter the narrow unnamed pathway opposite. Continue ahead to:

16. **Judges' Walk,** a pleasant path with a view that Constable loved. Many of his paintings depict variations of this vista (and some include imaginary houses, a windmill, and even Windsor Castle).

The Walk takes its name from the Great Plague of 1665, when city magistrates moved their court hearings outdoors to the edge of the heath in order to avoid possible exposure to infection from criminals and their accusers.

Don't walk on Judges' Walk. Instead, go through the small gap in the iron railing and continue along the rough pathway. Keep right until you reach Lower Terrace, where you should carefully cross to the center of the round-about and head to:

17. **Whitestone Pond,** a suburban lagoon named for a nearby white milestone that reads "4 miles from St. Giles pounds; 4½ miles from Holborn Barrs." When visiting his friend Leigh Hunt, who lived close by, poet Percy Bysshe Shelley (1792–1822) would come to this pond and sail paper boats with local children.

Walk toward the traffic lights and turn right onto Heath Street. Go down the left side of the street past the Friends Meeting House to the corner of Elm Row. The walled corner house is:

18. **1 Elm Row,** the home of author D. H. Lawrence (1885–1930) for several months during 1923. Lawrence's experiences in Hampstead inspired his short story "The Last Laugh."

Turn left onto Elm Row where, a few doors down on your left, is:

19. **3 Elm Row,** the former home of Sir Henry Cole. Cole, who founded the Victoria and Albert Museum, lived here from 1879 to 1880. Cole is also the person who originated the custom of sending Christmas cards.

Continue along Elm Row and turn left to Hampstead Square. Bear right across the square and continue straight to Cannon Place. Just ahead on the right is the clock-topped:

20. **Cannon Hall,** an 18th-century courthouse that was associated with the nearby Lock Up (see Stop 22). In the early 20th century, the hall was home to Sir Gerald du Maurier (1873–1934), father of writer Daphne du Maurier (*Rebecca*) and one of the last great turn-of-the-century actor/managers. Du Maurier made his mark with inspired interpretations of J. M. Barrie's plays and as the original Captain Hook in *Peter Pan*.

Around the corner are the three old **cannons** for which the hall and place are probably named. At one time the cannons served as hitching posts.

With your back to Cannon Hall, cross Cannon Lane and walk along Squires Mount. The row of cottages on your right is called:

21. **Squires Mount Croft.** Built in 1704, these are the oldest terrace homes in Hampstead.

   Retrace your steps to Cannon Hall and, with the wall on your right, continue three-quarters of the way down Cannon Place to the:

22. **Parish Lock Up,** 11 Cannon Place, an 18th-century jailhouse, one of only a few remaining in London. Before the government assumed responsibility for law enforcement, this was a function of local churches. This Parish Lock Up was built into the garden wall of Cannon Hall in the 1730s. The single dark cell was a holding pen where prisoners were kept until other arrangements could be made. Soon after the local police force was established in 1829, the Lock Up was moved to the Watchhouse in Holly Walk.

   At the bottom of the hill (now called Cannon Lane), cross Well Road and take the small pathway directly opposite to Well Walk. Turn right at the fountain. A few doors down on your left is:

23. **40 Well Walk,** the former home of John Constable. Constable lived here from 1827 until his death 10 years later. The artist's wife, Maria, developed pulmonary consumption soon after their seventh child was born, at the beginning of 1828. A friend who visited here shortly before Maria's death recalled how Constable appeared to be his usual self in his wife's presence. But later on, when the artist took him into another room, Constable burst into tears without speaking. Despite his sorrow, Constable maintained a caustic wit. Once he told the Hampstead dairyman, "In the future we shall feel obliged if you will send us the milk and the water in separate cans."

   Continue along Well Walk to the building next to the Wells Tavern. This is:

24. **1 Well Walk,** site of a former home of poet John Keats. He moved here with his brother, Tom, in 1817, the same year that his first volume of poems was published. The book's sales proved disappointing, however, and the publishers expressed regret over their involvement with Keats and his manuscript.

   Tom Keats was seriously ill while he lived here, and he relied on his brother to nurse him. Keats's friend and confidant Charles Armitage Brown wrote, "Early one morning I was awakened in my bed by a pressure on my hand. It was Keats who came to tell me his brother was no more. I said nothing . . . at length, my thoughts returned from the dead to the living. I said 'Have nothing more to do with those lodgings—and alone too. Had you not better live with me?' He paused, pressed my hand warmly, and replied, 'I think it would be better.'"

Keats soon moved into Brown's house, which was called Wentworth Place. Today it's better known as Keats's House (see Stop 27).

Cross Christchurch Hill and continue along Well Walk. At the iron fence, turn right onto New End Square and head to:

25. **Burgh House,** New End Square (☎ **0171/431-0144**), a fine Queen Anne home from 1703. The building was bought by Rev. Allatson Burgh in 1822, a minister who was accused of neglecting both his home and his congregation. Eventually the house came under control of the Burgh House Trust, which has established a small art museum here. The house is open Wednesday to Sunday from noon to 5pm. Admission is free.

Retrace your steps to Well Walk and continue straight ahead to Willow Road. Though this is a relatively long walk, the scenery is beautiful since much of the route runs along Hampstead Heath. Take your fourth right to:

26. **Downshire Hill,** one of the most bucolic streets in Hampstead. Nearly all the homes here are painstakingly preserved 19th-century structures.

Half a block to your right is the:

☕ **Take a Break**   **Freemasons Arms,** 32 Downshire Hill (☎ **0171/435-4498**), a spacious tavern known for its good lunches and gaming spirit. This is one of the few remaining places in London where skittles is still played. Somewhat like American 10-pin bowling, skittles entails tossing a heavy wooden disk at nine pins placed 20 feet away. Games are held on Tuesday, Thursday, and Saturday nights, and the pub offers a trophy to the "best newcomer."

Exit the pub, turn right, walk 1 block up Downshire Hill, and turn left to Keats Grove. Two blocks ahead on your right is:

27. **Keats's House** (Wentworth Place), Keats Grove (☎ **0171/ 435-2062**), the rather unassuming home where Romantic poet John Keats (1795–1821) lived and worked. The poet, who was very fond of Hampstead, wrote:

> *To one who has been long in city pent,*
> *'Tis very sweet to look into the fair*
> *And open face of heaven.*

This well-preserved Regency house is now open as a museum containing one of his first editions, as well as diaries, letters, assorted memorabilia, and some original furnishings. In April to October, Keats's House is open Monday to Friday from 10am to 1pm and 2 to 6pm, Saturday from 10am to 1pm and 2 to 5pm, and Sunday from 2 to 5pm. In November to March, it's open Monday to Friday from 1 to 5pm, Saturday from 10am to 1pm and 2 to 5pm, and Sunday from 2 to 5pm. Admission is free.

Continue along Keats Row and turn left onto Downshire Hill. Turn right onto Hampstead High Street, at the end of which is Hampstead Underground Station.

Essentials &
Recommended
Reading

GETTING AROUND

London can be a difficult city to negotiate. It seems as though no two streets run parallel, and even locals regularly consult maps. Construction sites further challenge walkers, but as you'll soon discover with this book, there's really no better way to go. In London, cars have the right-of-way over pedestrians; take care even when the light seems to be in your favor.

It's always best to cross streets at the end of a block in the areas designated for pedestrians ("zebra crossings"); always look to the *right* for oncoming cars (not to the left).

By Public Transportation

Commuters constantly complain about London's public transport, but visitors find the bus and tube networks both vast and efficient. Underground stations are abundant, and the red double-decker buses are fun to ride. Both systems are operated by London Regional Transport (LRT), which sets fares based on a zone system—you pay for each zone you cross.

London Regional Transport Travel Information Centres are located in the major Underground stations, including Heathrow, King's Cross, Oxford Circus, Piccadilly Circus, and Victoria. Off-hour times vary, but all provide service weekdays from 9am to 5pm. LRT also maintains a 24-hour information service at ☎ **0171/222-1234.**

You can save money by purchasing one of three types of **Travelcards.** A central London 1-day Travelcard is good for unlimited transportation within two zones on the bus and tube after 9:30am Monday to Friday and all day on weekends and public holidays. Weekly and monthly Travelcards are valid at all times. You'll need to present a photo to buy and use the weekly and monthly tickets; photo booths are located in most Underground stations.

By Underground

Except for Christmas Day, when the Underground is closed, the trains run every few minutes from about 5:30am on Monday to Saturday and from 7:30am on Sunday. Closing times vary with each station, but the last trains always leave between 11:30pm and midnight. The last train's departure time is posted at the entrance of each station. You can buy tickets from the station ticket window or at a nearby vending machine. Hold onto your ticket throughout your ride; you must present it when you reach your destination. Pick up a handy tube map, available free at station ticket windows. Note that there's an Underground map on the inside front cover of this book as well.

By Bus

It appears that the red open-back-platform buses will one day be a thing of the past; they're being replaced by the more economical driver-only type. But at least for now, you can still make a flying leap onto the departing vehicle. Take a seat, either upstairs or down, and wait for the conductor to collect your fare; since the fare will vary according to your destination, tell the conductor where you want to get off. On the newer type of bus, pay the driver as you enter and leave via the rear door.

Many visitors hesitate to ride the buses because their routes can be confusing. Get a free bus map from the tourist office or just ask any conductor about the route and enjoy a top-deck sightseeing adventure.

Like the tube, regular bus service stops after midnight. Night buses have different routes and numbers from their daytime counterparts, and service is less frequent. If you've just missed your night bus, expect a long wait for the next; you might prefer to look for a minicab (see below). The central London night-bus terminus is Trafalgar Square. One-day Travelcards (see above) aren't valid on night buses.

By Taxi

For three or four people traveling a short distance, black cabs can be economical. The city's big black cabs now come in other colors (primarily maroon), but the ride is still fun. Cabs are designed with a particularly tight turning radius, and there's enough interior room to accommodate a gentleman wearing a top hat. A taxi is available when the yellow sign on its roof is illuminated. Hail a cab by raising your arm. The driver will lower the window when he pulls to the curb so that you can state your destination before climbing in. You can hail a cab on the street or in front of train stations, large hotels, and popular attractions. If you know in advance that you'll need a cab, you can order one by calling ☎ **0171/272-0272.**

   Minicabs are meterless cars driven by licensed entrepreneurs. Technically, these taxis aren't allowed to cruise for fares but must operate from sidewalk offices—many of which are located around Leicester Square. Minicabs are handy after the tube shuts down for the night and black cabs suddenly become scarce. Always negotiate the fare beforehand, and if you're approached by a lone driver, hard bargaining is in order.

By Bicycle

Though there are no bike lanes and cars are unyielding, some people enjoy biking. If you want to rent a bike, try **On Your Bike,** 52–54 Tooley St., SE1 (☎ **0171/378-6669**), open Monday to Friday from 9am to 6pm and Saturday from 9:30am to 5:30pm.

By Car

It's not advisable to drive in the city; however, if you're planning some excursions, renting one is worthwhile. Inexpensive rental companies are **Practical Used Car Rental,** 111 Bartholomew Rd., NW5 (☎ **0171/284-0199**); **Avis** (☎ **0181/848-8733**);

and **Budget** (☎ **080/0626-063**). The last two have several branches throughout the city.

FAST FACTS London

Area Codes   The area code is **0171** in central London and **0181** in outer London. Area codes are necessary when dialing from outside the code area. From the United States, first dial the international access code, **011;** then the country code for England, **44;** then 171 or 181, respectively.

Banks   Most banks are open Monday to Friday from 9:30am to 3:30pm, but many stay open to 5pm and some are open Saturday from 9:30am to noon. They generally offer the best exchange rates, but American Express and Thomas Cook are competitive and don't charge a commission for cashing traveler's checks (even those of other financial institutions). American Express maintains several offices, including one at 6 Haymarket, SW1 (☎ **0171/930-8422**), near Trafalgar Square. A convenient Thomas Cook office is at 1 Marble Arch, W1 (☎ **0171/723-1668**). Both offices are open Monday to Friday from 9am to 5pm and Saturday from 9am to noon. Currency-exchange offices with the longest hours (sometimes open all night) tend to offer the least favorable rates. Beware of Chequepoint and other high-commission bureaux de change.

Bookstores   **Dillon's Bookstore,** 82 Gower St., WC1 (☎ **0171/636-1577**), in the heart of the university district, is one of London's largest and best chain bookstores. **Foyles,** 119 Charing Cross Rd., WC2 (☎ **0171/437-5660**), has a vast selection of illogically shelved titles. **Hatchards,** 187 Piccadilly, W1 (☎ **0171/437-3924**), an upscale bookshop, sells popular books and has a good travel section.

Business Hours   Stores are usually open Monday to Saturday from 10am to 6pm, but most stay open at least an additional hour one evening. The stores in Knightsbridge usually remain open to 7pm on Wednesday, and those in the West End stay open late on Thursday. Some shops around touristy Covent Garden stay open to 7 or 8pm every night. Most stores are closed on Sunday.

Currency   The pound sterling (£), a small, thick, round coin, is divided into 100 pence. Pence, often called "p," come in 1p, 2p,

5p, 10p, and 50p coins. Notes are issued in £5, £10, £20, and £50 denominations.

Embassies   The **U.S. Embassy,** 24 Grosvenor Sq., W1 (☎ **0171/499-9000**), is open to walk-in visitors Monday to Friday from 8:30 to 11am. The **Canadian High Commission,** Macdonald House, 1 Grosvenor Sq., W1 (☎ **0171/258-6600**), is open Monday to Friday from 9am to 5pm. The **Australian High Commission,** in Australia House on The Strand, WC2 (☎ **0171/379-4334**), is open Monday to Friday from 9am to 1pm. The **New Zealand High Commission,** in New Zealand House, 80 Haymarket, SW1 (☎ **0171/930-8422**), is open Monday to Friday from 9am to 5pm.

Emergencies   Police, fire, and ambulance services can be reached by dialing ☎ **999** from any phone. Coins aren't required.

Holidays   Most businesses are closed New Year's Day, Good Friday, Easter Monday, the first Monday in May, and December 25 and 26. In addition, many stores close on bank holidays, which are scattered throughout the year. There are no standard holidays for museums, restaurants, or sightseeing attractions. To avoid disappointment, always phone your intended destination before setting out.

Information   The London Tourist Board (LTB) staffs several information centers, including one in **Victoria Station's forecourt** (open daily: Easter–Oct 8am–7pm and Nov–Easter 9am–6pm) and in the basement of **Selfridges department store,** Oxford Street, W1 (open Mon–Wed 9:30am–7pm, Thurs–Fri 9:30am–8pm, and Sat 9:30am–6:30pm).

Mail   Post offices are plentiful and normally open Monday to Friday from 9am to 5pm and Saturday from 9am to noon. The **Main Post Office,** 24 William IV St., Trafalgar Square, WC2 (☎ **0171/930-9580**), is open Monday to Saturday from 8am to 8pm.

Newspapers/Magazines   There are many local newspapers in London. The listings magazine *Time Out* is indispensable for comprehensive information on what's happening in the city. There are newsstands outside virtually every tube station, and an unusually good selection of international newspapers and magazines is available at almost every little tobacco shop and food market.

Police   In an emergency, dial ☎ **999** from any phone; no coins are needed. At other times, dial the operator at ☎ **100** and ask to be connected with the police.

Taxes   Unlike in the United States, where a tax is added to your bill when you make a purchase, England's 17.5% **value-added tax (VAT)** is already included in the ticket price of most items for sale. Foreign tourists can reclaim the VAT for major purchases. Ask at department or specialty stores for details.

Telephone   London has two area codes: **0171** (for central London) and **0181** (for outer London). You need to use these codes only when phoning from outside the calling area. All phone numbers in this guide include area codes for your convenience—use them when applicable. For more, see "Area Codes" above.

There are normally two kinds of pay phone. The first accepts coins, while the other operates exclusively with a Phonecard, available from news agents in £1, £2, £4, £10, and £20 denominations. Phonecard telephones automatically deduct the price of your call from the card. To reach the local operator, dial ☎ **100.** The international operator is ☎ **155.** London information ("directory inquiries") can be reached by dialing ☎ **192** and is free from pay phones.

Tipping   Most (but not all) restaurants automatically add a discretionary service charge. The restaurant's policy will be explained on the menu. Where a service charge isn't included, a 10% to 15% tip is customary. Note that tipping is rare in pubs.

RECOMMENDED READING

Hundreds, perhaps thousands, of books have been written about London and thousands more about people who have lived there or still live there. We can read about the city through novels, plays, poems, histories, biographies, and guidebooks. Shakespeare and Dickens, two of Britain's best-known writers, exemplify those who can convey to us some idea of what London was like in earlier periods. We can also learn what everyday life was like and what concerned people through the works of such poets, playwrights, and novelists as William Blake, John Keats, Jane Austen, Emily and Charlotte Brontë, Lewis Carroll, George Eliot, and Oscar Wilde.

Virginia Woolf's *A Room of One's Own,* T.S. Eliot's *Wasteland,* and George Orwell's *Down and Out in Paris and London* are excellent literary windows into London's more recent past. London's social life is also evident in thousands of general-interest books, including some of the best mystery and suspense novels (for example, Sir Arthur Conan Doyle's Sherlock Holmes series and Agatha Christie's novels).

From an enormous number of books on and about London, I've chosen those that I believe represent the best.

Ackroyd, Peter, *Dickens' London: An Imaginative Vision* (Headline [UK], 1988).
A selection of fictional and personal writings of one of London's greatest authors, which presents a detailed picture of the city in the early 19th century.

Clout, Hugh, *The Times London History Atlas* (HarperCollins, 1991).
Street and regional maps, as well as historical information, from London's premier newspaper.

Doyle, Arthur Conan, *The Adventures and Memoirs of Sherlock Holmes* (Modern Library, 1946).
A colorful, textured view of late 19th-century London, encompassing fiction's best-loved detective.

George, M. Dorothy, *London Life in the Eighteenth Century* (Academy Chicago Publishers, 1985).
An enlightened and readable study of life in the Georgian period.

Graves, Robert, and Alan Hodge, *Long Weekend: A Social History of Great Britain, 1918–1939* (Norton, 1963).
A fascinating and straightforward account of Britain between the two World Wars.

Marshall, Dorothy, *Doctor Johnson's London* (Wiley, 1968).
Marshall re-creates the London that Dr. Johnson knew and loved, including its intellectual, literary, and artistic aspects.

Murrow, Edward R., *This Is London* (Schocken Books, 1989). London during World War II, as seen by the veteran CBS radio news reporter.

Pohl, Frederick Julius, *Like to the Lark: The Early Years of Shakespeare* (C. N. Potter, 1972). This book tries to reconstruct Shakespeare's "lost years" in London and answer many questions about his life.

Porter, Roy, *London: A Social History* (Harvard University Press, 1995). A book that focuses on the development of London during the past 400 years in light of the interests and commercial activities of its residents.

Richards, Timothy M., *City of London Pubs: A Practical and Historical Guide* (Drake Publishers, 1973). The author guides visitors and history buffs through the many infamous pubs that have played a significant role in London's past.

Schwartz, Richard B., *Daily Life in Johnson's London* (University of Wisconsin Press, 1983). An acclaimed scholarly study of London—city and society—in the mid-18th century.

Trease, Geoffrey, *London: A Concise History* (Scribner's, 1975). London's rich and varied past is examined from the heroic days of the Blitz, through the city's second fire, to the period of reconstruction that followed.

Waugh, Evelyn, *Brideshead Revisited* (Little, Brown, 1982). Set partially in the home counties around the city and abroad, this magnificent novel nonetheless describes to a tee London in the early 20th century.

Weinreb, Ben, and Christopher Hibbert (eds.), *The London Encyclopedia* (Adler & Adler, 1986). The definitive source for in-depth information on thousands of London buildings, institutions, and people.

Weintraub, Stanley, *The London Yankees: Portraits of American Writers and Artists in England, 1894–1914* (Harcourt Brace, 1979).
Weintraub focuses on the politicking and private lives of American authors and artists who spent considerable time in London prior to World War I.

West, Paul, *The Women of Whitechapel and Jack the Ripper* (Random House, 1991).
A fictional work that presents rich historical background information, as well as actual facts, pertaining to the most celebrated murder case in history.

Wilkes, John, *The London Police in the Nineteenth Century* (Lerner/Cambridge University Press, 1984).
The city, viewed from a unique perspective during its transition at the beginning of the Industrial Revolution.

Wilson, Jean M., *Virginia Woolf, Life and London: A Biography of Place* (Norton, 1988).
Twentieth-century London is explored, with special attention to the influence of the Bloomsbury circle of intellectuals and artists.

Also Worth the Read

Barker, Felix, London: *2,000 Years of a City and Its People* (Macmillan, 1974).

Beier, A. L., and Roger Finlay (eds.), *London Fifteen Hundred to Seventeen Hundred: The Making of the Metropolis* (Longman, 1986).

Bennett, Arnold, *London Life* (Ayer, 1976).

Betjeman, John, *Victorian & Edwardian London* (David & Charles, 1969).

Brewster, Dorothy, *Virginia Woolf's London* (Greenwood, 1979).

Brooke, Christopher, *London, 800–1216: The Shaping of a City* (University of California Press, 1975).

Cameron, Robert, and Alistair Cooke, *Above London* (Cameron, 1980).

Chancellor, Edwin B., *The London of Charles Dickens* (Gordon Press, 1976).

Davies, Andrew, *The Map of London: From 1746 to the Present Day* (David & Charles, 1988).

Defoe, Daniel, *Tour Thro' London About the Year 1725* (Ayer, 1929).

Ehrlich, Blake, *London on the Thames* (Little, Brown, 1966).

Ford, Ford Madox, *The Soul of London* (Haskell, 1972).

Gibson-Jarvie, Robert, *The City of London: A Financial & Commercial History* (Longwood Pub. Group, 1979).

Goodard, Donald, *Blimey! Another Book About London* (Quadrangle Books, 1972).

Hibbert, Christopher, *London: The Biography of a City* (Penguin, 1983).

James, Henry, *A London Life* (Arden, 1978).

Johnson, Samuel, *Johnson on Johnson: Personal Writings of Samuel Johnson* (Dutton, 1976).

Kirwan, Daniel J., *Palace and Hovel* (Abelard-Schuman, 1963).

Lejeune, Anthony, *The Gentlemen's Clubs of London* (Smith, 1979).

Manley, Lawrence, *London in the Age of Shakespeare* (Pennsylvania State University Press, 1987).

Olsen, Donald J., *The City As a Work of Art: London, Paris, Vienna* (Yale University Press, 1986).

Pepys, Samuel, *Everybody's Pepys: The Diary of Samuel Pepys 1660–1669* (Harcourt Brace, 1926).

Piper, David, *The Artist's London* (Oxford University Press, 1982).

Pritchett, Victor S., *London Perceived* (Harcourt Brace, 1966).

Swinnerton, Frank, *The Bookman's London* (R. West, 1980).

Thompson, John, *Orwell's London* (Schocken, 1985).

Timbs, John, *Clubs & Club Life in London with Anecdotes of Its Famous Coffee-Houses, Hostelries, & Taverns from the Seventeenth Century to the Present Time* (Gale, 1967).

Weightman, Gavin, and Steve Humphries, *The Making of Modern London.*

Woolf, Virginia, *The London Scene* (Hallman, 1975).

Index

FROMMER'S® COMPLETE TRAVEL GUIDES

*(Comprehensive guides to destinations around the world, with
selections in all price ranges—from deluxe to budget)*

FROMMER'S® PORTABLE GUIDES

*(Pocket-size guides for travelers who
want everything in a nutshell)*

FROMMER'S® DOLLAR-A-DAY GUIDES

(The ultimate guides to comfortable low-cost travel)

Australia from $50 a Day	Ireland from $50 a Day
California from $60 a Day	Israel from $50 a Day
Caribbean from $60 a Day	Italy from $50 a Day
Costa Rica & Belize from $35 a Day	London from $60 a Day
England from $60 a Day	Mexico from $35 a Day
Europe from $50 a Day	New York from $75 a Day
Florida from $50 a Day	New Zealand from $50 a Day
Greece from $50 a Day	Paris from $70 a Day
Hawaii from $60 a Day	San Francisco from $60 a Day
India from $40 a Day	Washington, D.C., from $60 a Day

FROMMER'S® AMERICA ON WHEELS

(Everything you need for a successful road trip, including full-color road maps and ratings for every hotel)

California & Nevada	Northwest & Great Plains
Florida	South-Central States & Texas
Great Lake States & Midwest	Southeast
Mid-Atlantic	Southwest
New England & New York	

FROMMER'S® MEMORABLE WALKS

(Memorable neighborhood strolls through the world's great cities)

Chicago	New York	San Francisco
London	Paris	Spain's Favorite Cities

FROMMER'S® NATIONAL PARK GUIDES

(Everything you need for the perfect park vacation)

Grand Canyon	Yosemite & Sequoia/Kings Canyon
National Parks of the American West	Zion & Bryce Canyon
Yellowstone & Grand Teton	

FROMMER'S® IRREVERENT GUIDES

(Wickedly honest guides for sophisticated travelers)

Amsterdam	New Orleans	Santa Fe
Chicago	Paris	Walt Disney World
London	San Francisco	Washington, D.C.
Manhattan		

FROMMER'S® BY NIGHT GUIDES

(The series for those who know that life begins after dark)

Amsterdam	Madrid & Barcelona	Paris
Chicago	Manhattan	Prague
Las Vegas	Miami	San Francisco
London	New Orleans	Washington, D.C.
Los Angeles		

SPECIAL-INTEREST TITLES

Arthur Frommer's
  New World of Travel
The Civil War Trust's Official Guide
  to the Civil War Discovery Trail
Frommer's Caribbean Hideaways
Frommer's Complete Hostel
  Vacation Guide to England,
  Scotland & Wales
Frommer's Europe's Greatest
  Driving Tours
Frommer's Food Lover's Companion
  to France
Frommer's Food Lover's Companion
  to Italy
Israel Past & Present
New York City with Kids
New York Times Weekends
Outside Magazine's Adventure Guide
  to New England

Outside Magazine's Adventure Guide
  to Northern California
Outside Magazine's Adventure Guide
  to the Pacific Northwest
Outside Magazine's Adventure Guide
  to Southern California & Baja
Outside Magazine's Guide
  to Family Vacations
Places Rated Almanac
Retirement Places Rated
Washington, D.C., with Kids
Wonderful Weekends from
  New York City
Wonderful Weekends from San
  Francisco
Wonderful Weekends from Los
  Angeles

THE COMPLETE IDIOT'S TRAVEL GUIDES

(The ultimate user-friendly trip planners)

Cruise Bacations	New York City	San Francisco
Las Vegas	Planning Your Trip to	Walt Disney World
New Orleans	Europe	

UNOFFICIAL GUIDES

*(Get the unbiased truth from these
candid, value-conscious guides)*

Atlanta	The Great Smoky &	New York City
Branson, Missouri	Blue Ridge	San Francisco
Chicago	Mountains	Skiing in the West
Cruises	Las Vegas	Walt Disney World
Disneyland	Miami & the Keys	Walt Disney World
	Mini-Mickey	Companion
	New Orleans	Washington, D.C.

FROMMER'S® DRIVING TOURS

*(Four-color photos and detailed maps
outlining spectacular scenic driving routes)*

America	France	New England
Britain	Germany	Scotland
California	Ireland	Spain
Florida	Italy	Western Europe